GOSPEL SHAPED EMOTIONS

*Learning to Lay Our Emotions
Down at the Cross of Jesus*

KEVIN WILSON

WESTBOW
PRESS®
A DIVISION OF THOMAS NELSON
& ZONDERVAN

Copyright © 2019 Kevin Wilson.

All rights reserved. No part of this book may be used or reproduced by any means, graphic, electronic, or mechanical, including photocopying, recording, taping or by any information storage retrieval system without the written permission of the author except in the case of brief quotations embodied in critical articles and reviews.

This book is a work of non-fiction. Unless otherwise noted, the author and the publisher make no explicit guarantees as to the accuracy of the information contained in this book and in some cases, names of people and places have been altered to protect their privacy.

WestBow Press books may be ordered through booksellers or by contacting:

WestBow Press
A Division of Thomas Nelson & Zondervan
1663 Liberty Drive
Bloomington, IN 47403
www.westbowpress.com
1 (866) 928-1240

Because of the dynamic nature of the Internet, any web addresses or links contained in this book may have changed since publication and may no longer be valid. The views expressed in this work are solely those of the author and do not necessarily reflect the views of the publisher, and the publisher hereby disclaims any responsibility for them.

Any people depicted in stock imagery provided by Getty Images are models, and such images are being used for illustrative purposes only.
Certain stock imagery © Getty Images.

Unless otherwise indicated, all Scripture quotations have been taken from the Christian Standard Bible®, Copyright © 2017 by Holman Bible Publishers. Used by permission. Christian Standard Bible® and CSB® are federally registered trademarks of Holman Bible Publishers.

Scripture quotations marked (ESV) are from the ESV® Bible (The Holy Bible, English Standard Version®), copyright © 2001 by Crossway, a publishing ministry of Good News Publishers. Used by permission. All rights reserved.

ISBN: 978-1-9736-7097-1 (sc)
ISBN: 978-1-9736-7098-8 (hc)
ISBN: 978-1-9736-7096-4 (e)

Library of Congress Control Number: 2019910862

Print information available on the last page.

WestBow Press rev. date: 8/5/2019

To my wife, Kristina Wilson

Thanks for loving me with patience and grace
while the gospel shapes my emotions.

"And be kind and compassionate to one another, forgiving
one another, just as God also forgave you in Christ."
—Ephesians 4:32

Contents

Preface		ix
1	Out-of-Control Emotions and the War Within	1
2	When Our Emotions Are Stronger than Our Convictions	7
3	The Chasm Between Feeling and Knowing	13
4	Our Emotions May Seem Big, but God Is Bigger	17
5	Gospel-Shaped Emotions	23
6	Why Am I So Angry?	29
7	When Can I Be Angry?	35
8	How the Gospel Shapes Our Anger	41
9	Slowing Down Our Anger	45
10	Understanding the Righteousness of God	51
11	The Weight of Anxiety	57
12	Hidden in the Shadow of the Almighty	63
13	Dining in the Presence of the Enemy	69
14	A Better Way	75
15	The Antidote for an Anxious Life	81
16	Where Does Joy Originate?	87
17	When Joy Withers	93
18	When You Fight for Your Joy and the Joy of Others	99
19	Finding Joy in Suffering	105

20	Rooted in Joy	111
21	When Grief Shows Up	117
22	The Grief of Loss	123
23	The Grief Over Sin	129
24	Grieving Over Lostness	135
25	The Grief of Jesus	143
Conclusion		149
Endnotes		155

Preface

The apostle Paul writes the following: "For I do not understand what I am doing, because I do not practice what I want to do, but I do what I hate" (Romans 7:15). I have experienced this dilemma in my spiritual life on more than occasion. I take two steps forward in devotion and allegiance to the Lord, only to blow it, taking two steps back. Seemingly, there is always tension between believing and obeying the way you ought and falling flat on your face, doing something you hate. I have been a believer for thirty-four years, and one would think the gulf between following Jesus faithfully and failing miserably in my walk with him would be quite wide, yet in my experience, this gulf can be paper thin.

Often my emotions are an indicator of how thin this gulf is. My emotions come out of nowhere, seizing control of the situation before I even know what is happening. Our emotions are complex, allowing humanity to express the heart and mind in ways we can't imagine. And here is where the trouble often begins. Our emotions are like temperature gauges, registering the conditions of our hearts, showing us and the world what is going on deep down in the bottom of our souls.

Emotions are not bad, in and of themselves; they serve to show what is going on in our lives. We use them to express ourselves, but often they can get the better of us and take us down a path we never intended to go. Several things can shape our emotions. Family, friends, finances, and circumstances all can affect how we view the world and finally how we express how we view the world. How many times have I said the right thing but with the wrong tone? How many times have I felt anxiety steal a moment or attach joy to an object that should have never given me joy? How often has grief stayed too long or anger destroyed a relationship so quickly?

The chapters that follow are not written from a physiological point of view. This work is not intended to diagnose what is going on in your brain or even how this affects the emotions you experience. Many suffer from chemical imbalance, and God has given us professional counselors and guides as a help. The whole purpose of this book is to help the local church find a safe place for their emotions, and this place is not a place at all—he's a person.

In Jesus, I have found someone who sees my anger, understands what is going on in my heart, and patiently helps me control and shape the anger I experience. In Jesus, I have found a King who is sovereign over all aspects of creation, even the small details of my life. In Jesus, I have found a friend who listens to my worries and lovingly allows me to lay the burdens of life that can cause so much anxiety at his loving feet. In Jesus, I have found a God who not only brings me joy but who has endured the wrath of God poured out on the cross with joy on my behalf.

Our emotions need to go the way of the cross. Our emotions can be shaped by an eternal being who rules the universe while taking care of the needs we bring before him. Our emotions are complex, and this work will not address everything that controls our emotions, but it will direct the reader down a path that leads to a God who not only saves us from our sin but can save us from our emotions. My prayer is that material contained in these pages is saturated in the gospel and helps to guide the emotions of the reader toward the wonderfulness of our Lord. They are not my words alone; I want to thank Chris Moses and Chris and Barbara Conner for their word choice, wisdom, guidance, and words of encouragement during this process. Their help has shaped much of what is written, and I am thankful for their help and contribution.

CHAPTER 1
Out-of-Control Emotions and the War Within

*What causes quarrels and what causes fights among you?
Is it not this, that your passions are at war within you?*
—James 4:1 (ESV)

My wife and I waited a while before having our first child. We wanted to travel, do ministry together, and get to know each other before children came into the picture. Even with these goals, it wasn't too long until we began to long for our family to grow. And then it happened. Or I should say *she* happened. In the fall of 2008, the Lord provided a child—a little girl, so petite and vulnerable. I awoke the first night at every distinct sound that filled the room where now there were three instead of two. I remember placing her in the car to take her home and driving so slowly over each impending speed bump, wanting to keep her safe from the outside world we were entering. There we were, the perfect little family, setting off on a journey of a lifetime. We were two parents blessed by God and ready for this new life.

Days were filled with short nights, 2:00 a.m. feedings, and a lot of dirty diapers. In the midst of the chaos, we began to cherish and love this little girl. The smell of her hair, the way she giggled and smiled when she woke up from a nap, and the way she gripped my fingers quickly captured my heart. My mind still recalls the way she would sneeze and then let out an *ahh* after this explosion that would rock her tiny body. I would not trade those days for anything in the world, although there were moments we thought would break us, moments that tested our marriage and our faith. Those moments stretched us to the point of breaking, thus sending our emotions spiraling out of control. They made us think we were losing our minds and sensibility.

I recall times when it seemed I was not in control of anything, including the emotions I was experiencing daily. My wife, Kristina, and I marched into these days armed with a litany of schedules, books, and planners. Our tired bodies would not give in, and we would not give up. We read books, received advice from others who had traveled this road before, and consulted doctors and specialists along the way. Armed with these resources, we couldn't fail. We were in control of the situation.

I worked only a mile or so away from our house. I could slip in and out to check on my girls, grab the occasional lunch, and sometimes allow Kristina to escape for a quick grocery run. One day when I left the office to come home to see my girls, the house was silent. My greetings of "Daddy's home!" seemed to fall on deaf ears. The house was quiet; all I could hear were my footsteps as I plodded across the kitchen floor.

I found my way to the second floor and then the entrance to the nursery, a room with four large yellow letters spelling the word BABY hanging over a crib. The crib was decorated with tons of animals. Unclean and clean alike crowded into a tiny boat with a little guy carrying a staff. He resembled Gandalf from *The Lord of the Rings* instead of Noah. In the midst of this fun-filled environment we had tried to create with furniture, signs, and biblical characters aplenty sat an exhausted mother and daughter, both in tears, drained from a long day of out-of-control emotions. I am a pastor; I always have something to say, but I couldn't find the words. Anna Kate, our daughter, lay in her mom's lap, crying uncontrollably. I could tell by the exhausted look on Kristina's face and the tears rolling down her cheeks that this had been going on for a while. Both my loves were experiencing out-of-control emotions, and I didn't have a clue what to do or say.

Emotions take us places never imagined. They help us express ourselves, showing others how joyful life is or how awful our experiences are. But what happens when we experience these emotions and they seem to be in control of us? What happens when anger, fear, grief, or sadness completely dominates our outlook on life and the lives of others? What happens when life seems to cave in under the pressures we experience, and our emotions lash out, leading us down a path we never thought we would take? Emotions help us express ourselves, but they can also be a window into our hearts. The prophet Jeremiah describes the human heart with these words: "The heart is deceitful above all things, and desperately sick; who can understand it?"

(Jeremiah 17:9 ESV). The emotions we experience come from a heart that is expressing itself in a fallen world. Daily, we fight a war for our souls, and often our emotions help us to see how we are fighting, but does this mean that our emotions are bad?

Emotions Are Not the Problem

We all experience emotions daily. The emotions we experience are not intrinsically evil or sinful in themselves, but when these emotions get out of control, they tend to lead us to places we never thought we would go. Often our emotions are out of control when they outrun our brains, meaning our minds can't keep up with and process the emotions we are experiencing. The problem is our renegade hearts. We have hearts that are sinful to the core. They rebel against God, his grace, his goodness, and his people. You see, the problem we have is not that we are too emotional or that we experience myriad emotions in the general occurrence of life. The problem is with us. It's the way we process the world around us as sinners. We have a problem, and it will affect the way we, as sinful creatures, experience the world God has created.

James addresses this issue in chapter 4 of his epistle. James writes these words describing what out-of-control emotions tend to lead to: "What cause quarrels and what causes fights among you? Is it not this, that your passions are at war among you?" (James 4:1 ESV).

James identifies that the major cause of conflict within and without is linked to the out-of-control passions and desires of the human heart. These lead to out-of-control emotions that can snowball into a frenzy of hurt feelings, misconstrued words, and damaged relationships that take years to rebuild, even if each party wants to start the reconciliation process. So we fight and quarrel, fueled by out-of-control emotions, and the resentment from others builds. Think about it. How many words ruin relationships when an out-of-control emotion like anger leads to rage and harsh words? Take, for instance, my marriage. Sometimes I can't even remember why I am angry, yet my emotions run loose and unbridled, which often leads to hurtful words and actions aimed straight at the character and personhood of my beloved. Or what about when our fear of the unknown grips our hearts so tightly that we experience a paralysis of life? It becomes a point where the rational decision-making process ends up being thwarted by the fear of what is around the next corner.

As said earlier, we experience emotions daily. The question is this: are we in control of our emotions, or are our emotions in control of us?

I must make a personal confession: often, I'm not in control of anything, including my emotions! The most natural remedy for many of us would be to try harder with our emotions—to find a technique that helps. We could take a yoga class to help with our anxiety, or practice counting backward from ten to damper our anger before it gets out of control. I think most of us have been told to "get over" something or to not be so emotional with our decisions. We search for a behavior or technique to help us cope, when behavior modification is more often a Band-Aid than a remedy.

I'm not saying that we are not responsible for our emotions or our actions. Of course, we can make rational decisions outside of the emotions we experience. I am saying, however, that the emotions we experience are often real and seem more significant than the problem or obstacle we are facing. We don't need to stop being emotional. We need something—or someone—more meaningful than our emotions.

Jesus makes an incredible statement to his present and future followers in the gospel of Matthew. In Matthew 28:18, Christ leaves his followers with these words: "All authority in heaven and on earth has been given to me" (ESV). Everything we do as believers is rooted in the resurrected Lord's bold statement concerning the reality of his presence. Everything in heaven and earth is under his rule and authority. Every experience the disciples will face passes through the unchanging hand of *the* risen Lord—even the emotions they will experience daily. What does this mean for us? It says that the church has an anchor for our out-of-control emotions, and his name is Wonderful Counselor, Mighty God, Prince of Peace, the Alpha and Omega, Everlasting Father, the Ancient of Days, the Son of God, and the Lamb of God who takes away the sins of the world!

You see, we need something more significant than our emotions. We find this more significant object in God and in the attributes that define who he is as we experience him. We need to lose our emotions. We should not stuff them or hide them, but we should lose them in Christ and his attributes, knowing he can swallow up out-of-control emotions and subject them to the reign and control of Christ.

Go back to that day in Anna Kate's nursery. Kristina and I were experiencing a lot of out-of-control emotions. Anna Kate was an infant; all we could do was provide for her needs and comfort her. I could have looked at my wife and said, "Get a grip. Don't be so emotional. Go and find your happy place." But she was overwhelmed by the emotions we were all experiencing. I could have stuffed my emotions and said, "Daddy is going to make everything better; don't worry. I'm home now." But my presence wasn't making a dent in the emotions she was experiencing. However, we could look to one greater than what we were experiencing at the current moment; one who has conquered not only death and the grave but is alive and abides with us. We could look to him, and, as the psalmist instructs us in Psalm 46:10, "Be still and know that I am God" (ESV). The following pages and chapters will look to anchor the reader in the everlasting truth of the gospel of Jesus Christ and that by knowing him and abiding in his presence, we will find that our emotions find themselves at his feet as well.

Questions for Personal Reflection

1. Who or what currently controls your emotions?
2. How are you allowing out-of-control emotions and matters to control your life?
3. What do you sense God saying to you regarding the way your process your emotions?

CHAPTER 2
When Our Emotions Are Stronger than Our Convictions

In those days there was no king in Israel. Everyone did what was right in his own eyes.
—Judges 17:6 (ESV)

I like it when I am right. When I believe in a certain position that I take on a subject, I can make a compelling argument in my own heart and mind for my justification. Others may try to persuade me to take another side, but over time, I have built a foundation of convictions on which my actions, thoughts, attitudes, and heart are set. I have constructed these convictions over some years, and the people I trust have helped to shape them, but primarily it's the faith I have in Christ.

We all have a worldview—this is how we look at and interact with the world around us. Our worldview shapes how we look at people and the circumstances in which we find ourselves. Our worldview also develops the convictions we hold. I am a Christian, so my beliefs are anchored in the gospel of Jesus Christ and the authority and sufficiency of the scriptures, where God has revealed the story of redemption. Primarily, the Bible has shaped my convictions regarding some of the most critical questions in life, such as, "Who am I? What is my purpose in life? How did I get here?"

People throughout history have asked these questions, and as a result,

> I have constructed these convictions over some years, and the people I trust have helped to shape them, but primarily it's the faith I have in Christ.

humanity has developed fundamental convictions regarding the underlying structural issues in life. Some of these convictions are based on moral stances, some on cultural attitudes, and others on personal preferences. The question the Christian must ask is twofold. First, from where will the basis for my convictions come? Second, how will my emotions respond to the beliefs I have?

Let's look at the connection between our convictions and our emotions.

The Connection Between Our Convictions and Emotions

I stated earlier that our convictions help shape how we see the world around us. I am not saying they are the only things that shape our worldview. Culture, circumstances, and our relationships also can develop our worldview, yet our convictions constitute a significant building block to the way we view the world.

As Christians, we are to hold our convictions in balance with our emotions. In Ephesians 4:26, Paul instructs the church at Ephesus to "be angry and do not sin; do not let the sun go down on your anger" (ESV). Paul is stating that we can have an emotion—anger—yet this anger can have boundaries, formed by convictions ("do not sin"), which flow from a Christian worldview, shaped by the gospel of Jesus Christ.

So Paul is saying there are times when we can have the emotion of anger, and this anger can be regulated by the convictions of our hearts—that we do not sin against the God of heaven or our fellow neighbor. Paul even gives a timeline on this process. He urges his readers not to let a day pass until they live out their convictions not to sin and restore the relationship with the brother who has caused them to have the emotion of anger.

Sounds simple, right? In my experience, this process is not that simple. Why? Because my emotions often scream louder than my convictions, and they end up getting their way.

Remember what James had to say in chapter 4 of his epistle. Desires of the heart want to have sway over our behavior and attitudes. I can *know* it is wrong to allow my anger to get the best of me and cause me to sin. I can *recognize* it is wrong for me to let things fester within my heart until

> Because my emotions often scream louder than my convictions, and they end up getting their way.

they bubble up on the surface and explode into a rage or descend into a bitter attitude toward the person or situation that has angered me. It has been my experience—and probably yours as well—that my convictions do not win out when faced with an out-of-control emotion. That does not mean that the beliefs we have, especially as Christians, are fake, weak, or misguided. It does say they are not as strong as the emotions we feel at present.

As affirmed earlier, our convictions end up being shaped by different variables. Two of the most important variables that shape convictions are the relationships we have and the things we believe. As a Christian, there are certain truth propositions I believe. The scriptures outline these foundational core beliefs, shaping what a Christian believes. Jesus is the Son of God, and we find salvation, forgiveness of sins, and fellowship in the sacrifice of Christ. Christians throughout time have developed creeds and documents that have outlined their convictions, which are rooted in the truth of scriptures.

My relationships also build my beliefs. Pastors, small-group leaders, deacons, elders, and seminary professors have shaped the way I view God. My parents had the most influence on my spiritual life. My father and mother taught me critical principles on how to conduct myself and treat others. My parents were believers, so their faith influenced many of the principles they handed down to me.

When what we believe does not correlate with how we behave, we have a problem. Often, our emotions take our actions to a place we never intended to go. This reaction happens when we feel our convictions threatened. We don't want to let our emotions get the best of us, yet they push on our convictions, and our feelings come out. For example, your child disobeys. Your conviction is that your child should obey you, as well as other authority figures and the rules they have in place. Your child continues to push, and you push back until you lose your temper, and your emotions control your behavior instead of your convictions. What about when fear takes over? You know, as a Christian, that God is your protector and provider. Certain convictions have shaped this view of God, mainly the scriptures and the community you find in the relationships you have in the local church. Then a circumstance happens that you were not expecting. You get the phone call no one wants to answer; you lose your job; your marriage crumbles—and instantly, the emotion of fear takes over. You find yourself waking up at night, fearful of what the day holds. You dread the next text, email, or phone call, knowing that it could bring bad news. Emotions are powerful; they can paralyze and lead to unwise decisions when they trump the convictions we have as Christians. What do we do?

Bringing Our Emotions to the King

In the Old Testament book of Judges, we see a big problem. The text of Judges is cyclical, meaning the people of Israel do the same thing over and over, never learning from their mistakes. The cycles go like this: the people of God are unfaithful to their covenant relationship to God. Because of their unbelief and unfaithfulness, God delivers them to their enemies. The people cry out to God for help; God sends someone, in the form of a judge, who delivers them from their situation and sin. Time passes, and they repeat the cycle.

Insanity is doing the same thing over and over and expecting different results. The book of Judges is a case study on just that—doing the same thing over and over and expecting different results. Why would the people of God continue in this cycle? We find the answer in Judges 17:6. "In those days there was no king in Israel. Everyone did what was right in his own eyes" (ESV). God's people had an identity crisis. They identified with the commands and rules Moses gave to them in the law of God, yet their convictions gave way to their desires. These desires influenced their emotions.

We see this throughout the scriptures. Gideon doubts the provision of God, Barak is fearful of invading armies, Samson gives in to his lust and reveals the secret to his strength—the list goes on and on. Uncontrolled desires and emotions lead to forgotten convictions, and the people of God are under the sway of sin.

> Insanity is doing the same thing over and over and expecting different results.

Why? Because people did what they wanted, and there was no king in Israel. We need our convictions and our emotions under a king—not just any king but the King of kings. The man Jesus is the answer, and his gospel delivers us from ourselves, giving us the ability to keep the convictions we have and our emotions in check. How does he do this? Our feelings can find a safe place in the rule and reign of Jesus. Philippians 2:9 states this concerning Jesus:

> Therefore God has highly exalted him and bestowed on him the name that is above every name, so that at the name of Jesus every knee should bow, in heaven and on earth, and under the earth, and every tongue confess that Jesus Christ is Lord, to the glory of God the Father. (ESV)

You see, Jesus is highly exalted because he endured the cross for the elect found in Christ. Sinners are set free from the bondage and death of their old lives, and they can now live freely under the reign of a kind and wise King Jesus. *Jesus is better than anything in life, and his rule shapes how we see the world.* Everything can be subject to him, including our emotions. Which emotions need to come under his control today?

> Jesus is better than anything in life, and his rule shapes how we see the world.

Questions for Personal Reflection

1. What convictions serve as your foundation for living?
2. Who has influenced your convictions and worldview?
3. Which emotion(s) does God want you to bring to him? Why?

CHAPTER 3
The Chasm Between Feeling and Knowing

That I may know him and the power of his resurrection, and may share his suffering, becoming like him in his death.
—Philippians 3:10 (ESV)

Our feelings often betray us. Our emotions can lead us to erroneous conclusions regarding circumstances in which we find ourselves and the people with whom we interact each day. I find myself guilty of allowing a certain feeling I get to dictate how I respond to everyday life. I may feel uncomfortable in a certain situation and have often allowed this feeling to direct the choices that face me. Let me explain: have you ever encountered a stranger on the sidewalk who has made you feel uncomfortable? I have, and more than once I have avoided eye contact, walked the other way, or hurried past that person in an attempt to get out of the situation. Why? Because I had a certain feeling and allowed that feeling to influence my behavior, even without knowing the truth of the circumstance in which I found myself. Now please hear me: I am *not* saying you shouldn't be wise or that you should ignore your gut in a situation. I am not advocating a laissez-faire approach to life or throwing caution to the wind when it comes to certain situations and encounters. However, I do believe we allow feelings and emotions to dictate our actions instead of the truth of the particular situation.

There can be a larger-than-life chasm between what we know to be true and what we may feel about a situation. Now, should we be cautious in using our judgment when we do not see the truth of a situation? Absolutely! Many believers know what truth is but refuse to walk in the truth because their feelings hold them at bay.

What Is Truth?

John records an astonishing conversation between our Lord and Pilate:

> "You are a king then?" Pilate asked. "You say that I'm a king," Jesus replied. "I was born for this, and I have come into the world for this; to testify to the truth. Everyone who is of the truth listens to my voice." "What is the truth?" said Pilate. (John 18:37–38)

Pilate and Jesus were on two sides of what truth is. Jesus makes a bold proclamation in John 18:37: "I have come into the world for this; to testify to the truth. Everyone who is of the truth listens to my voice." Jesus does not mince words. His mission was to proclaim the truth. His birth, life, ministry, and, ultimately, his death and resurrection would be a testimony to the truth of all things. *In Jesus, we find all the answers to life's biggest questions.* His gospel, his voice, his words, and his life all point to the answer Pilate is seeking; namely, "What is the truth?"

Even though Jesus is on trial, he is entirely in control. His words have power and hope. Where can we go when truth seems out of reach? We can go to Jesus. Where can we go when our life is out of control? We can go to Jesus. What words do we need to hear to comfort and bring peace to a world of chaos? We need to listen to the words of Jesus and experience his gospel power. Pilate had the answer in front of him, yet he chose to pose the question, "What is the truth?"

> In Jesus, we find all the answers to life's biggest questions.

I think a lot of us, including me, are stuck where Pilate finds himself. We believe Jesus will save, protect, guide, and lead. We have placed our faith in the promise of who he is. However, our feelings tell us something different. They object to his plan, provision, and peace. If we are not careful, our emotions will lead us away from the truth of the gospel, which is the foundation for our very hope and faith, and convince us there is another way, thus creating a massive chasm between what we should *know* as Christians and what we *feel* in our present states. What are we to do? Questioning the truth of the sovereign Lord is not the answer. Paul, however, gives us a better way.

When Feeling Gives Way to Knowing

I was in Cub Scouts as a boy. I only lasted one year, but I can remember enjoying the projects, badges, and trips I took as a scout. One day, our leaders took us on a field trip. Our destination was the county jail, a place I had only driven by on the way to the local drive-in theater. (Yes, this was a while ago!) I can still remember the feeling and emotions I had as we entered the jail. We entered a small cinderblock room painted a very dull gray. Plastic red chairs lined the small area, and a large steel door stood in front of us. An ominous buzzer sounded, and a single red light brightly burned above this door as my troop walked into the inner sanctum of the jail. The lights were dimmed and were the only illumination as we faced four separate jail cells. My emotions were running wild, and all I wanted to do was leave. (Maybe that was why I never made it past my first year in scouts.)

One of the prisoners, an older gentleman, spoke up. I will always remember his words: "Don't make the choices I made. Listen to your parents." I think I was a perfect child for the next six months of my life. I learned two things from that field trip: (1) I didn't want to revisit a jail, and (2) I hated the way I felt while I was there. I wanted out of that environment.

Paul writes to the Philippian church from a jail cell. This jail cell was unlike the one I saw. He was chained to a Roman guard. The cell he was held captive in could have been a cave or other holding. Yet, Paul makes a profound statement: "That I may know him and the power of his resurrection, and may share his sufferings becoming like him in his death" (Philippians 3:10 ESV). Paul's basis of belief was not wrapped up in his judgments or the emotions he experienced; instead, his desires were anchored securely by his knowledge of Jesus Christ. He wanted more of that knowledge. Paul made a decision to feed his knowledge of Christ, which overshadowed his jail cell.

This knowledge was rooted in the power of the resurrection. Paul found his present life made sense because his old life was made new in Christ. His current circumstances bowed to the power of the resurrection and the authority and knowledge of Christ. Paul's worldview was different from the nation of Israel's worldview in the book of Judges.

Israel was led by their passions and their understanding of the world around them. Whatever they saw fit to do in their "own eyes," they did, without seeking or understanding the law of God, the person of God or the nature of God. In a sense, they desired self-rule instead of allowing their motives, desires, and actions to be under the rule of the God of the universe. Paul, on the other hand, completely trusted God with whatever happened. His circumstances, although very real and very inconvenient, could not take his heart away from the knowledge of God and the plan he had for Paul.

Too often I find myself more confident in my own rule and reign than the provision and plan of Jesus. What should we do when we see ourselves putting more confidence in ourselves, our emotions, and our circumstances than in the gospel of Jesus? We must repent. Many of us see repentance as a one-time event attached to a fixed time in our experiences, mainly our conversions. This understanding of repentance is only half right. Repentance is a daily posture before the King's throne. We boldly approach his throne of grace, bowed down before the King, with our backs turned from our old lives to abide by the new life. As believers, we have no time for self-governing because a new King has our hearts.

> Repentance is a daily posture before the King's throne.

So how do you span the chasm between the knowledge you have in Christ and the present emotions you may feel? How do you worship the King, even when you don't feel like it? You realize that his character is big enough to handle your situation and your emotions.

> Too often I find myself more confident in my own rule and reign than the provision and plan of Jesus.

Questions for Personal Reflection

1. How have your feelings betrayed you and led you away from Christ?
2. Slowly read Philippians 3:10 and consider each word. What about this verse confuses, frightens, or challenges you?
3. What does repentance look like in your life?

CHAPTER 4
Our Emotions May Seem Big, but God Is Bigger

Remember the former things of old; for I am God, and there is no other; I am God, and there is none like me, declaring the end from the beginning and from ancient times things not yet done, saying 'My counsel shall stand and I will accomplish my purpose.
—Isaiah 46:9–10 (ESV)

One of the reasons our emotions get out of control is because they seem more significant than they are. Our feelings seem more significant because the trigger point of those emotions, usually a circumstance, appears more prominent than it is. For instance, your sweet two-year-old draws on your antique furniture and ruins it. This is unfortunate but not life-changing, and the world certainly has not stopped rotating on its axis because of this mishap. But you lose it! There is no restraint as emotions flood from your head to your heart, and finally, they find your behavior and actions. You lose your temper, and anyone or anything in the path of this out-of-control emotion takes the brunt of your rage. Yes, I said anything. Have you ever taken your anger out on an object? I have, even though the inanimate object didn't intend to push my buttons or get my emotions fired up.

The situation controls you because at that moment, it consumes you. You get lost in your world, which is ruled by your own emotions, which react to your present circumstances—and so the cycle goes on again. We need something or someone who is more significant than our emotions. We need our feelings to back down and find their rest in someone who can guide and control them. Our emotions are good; God made us as emotional beings. Our feelings need to be checked by one who is bigger and more powerful than anything else. Christians find this one in the God of the entire universe. This God is the all-present, all-powerful supreme being of the cosmos, and we have a relationship with him through his only begotten Son, Jesus Christ. Why do believers find rest from their emotions in the God of the universe? Because he has disclosed who he is, and we can have confidence that he is what he says he is.

We learn who God is and about his character from the pages of scripture. God declares who he is throughout the Bible, which speaks of his character—his nature. Essentially, his attributes are who he says he is.

Not Like Us

You can know God by his incommunicable attributes. These attributes witness to humanity how God is different from us. God is all-powerful; we are not. God is all-knowing; we are not. God is independent; we are not. God also communicates who he is through his communicable attributes, which testify to how we are like God in certain ways. God is gracious, and we can be gracious as well. God is love, and we are called to love one another. God can grant mercy, and we are instructed to be merciful as well. God is not the sum of his attributes, and these attributes are not additions to his actual being. Christians serve a trinitarian God, meaning he is Father, Son, and Holy Spirit—one in essence but three in person. The Father is not the Son; the Son is not the Father; the Son is not the Holy Spirit; and the Holy Spirit is not the Father, and so on. God is one in being, with the same attributes or character.

He is unchanging in his attributes and decrees, and we are not. We are tossed to and fro by the choices we make, the situations in which we find ourselves, and the emotions that too often can run amok as we navigate life. These emotions, which God has generously given us, can find a hiding place in the attributes of this eternal God.

The Incommunicable Attributes of God

Throughout scripture, we see ways in which God is not like us. As mentioned earlier, these are his incommunicable attributes, which God does not share with humanity. These attributes are his independence, his omnipresence, his unity, and that he is unchanging and eternal. There is no way to understand God based on these categories alone, but we have to start somewhere, and once we see who God is through his attributes, then we will trust him more when our emotions go rogue. I won't address all of his incommunicable attributes here, but let's look at one of them; namely, his immutability—that God is unchanging.

God's Immutability

God has disclosed that he does not change in respect to his being, his purposes, and his promises, and we can trust that.

> Every good gift and every perfect gift is from above, coming down from the Father of lights, with whom there is no variation or shadow due to change. (James 1:17 ESV)

We can trust that God's being never changes and that he will keep giving his good gifts of grace. He will never stop; there will always be a supply of these good gifts of God. What does this mean for you and me? It means that even though our emotions are not constant, he is constant. It means that when we are overwhelmed, he is not. It means that when we feel defeated, he does not. Our emotions change all the time, but we can find peace because his being is constant and steady.

God also does not change his purposes. We humans have always tried to "find" ourselves. We go through a midlife crisis and finally find our real purpose in life, so we switch careers or take up new hobbies. We may abandon relationships, friendships, dreams, and even marriages to find our purposes in life. People have said things to me such as, "I have found myself now," even though the unwise decisions they made were not rooted in scripture. Many times, well-meaning, Christ-following believers base major decisions on a fleeting emotion or feeling, which ends up having disastrous consequences they never saw coming. Why? Because we are fickle creatures who often are blind to our own purposes, let alone the purposes of an eternal God. God is not like us in this respect. Once he decrees a purpose, it is unchanging and will come to pass.

> My counsel shall stand, and I will accomplish my purpose.
> (Isaiah 46:10 ESV)

You and I may abandon the purpose we knew was right and pursue something entirely against our convictions and God's purposes. We need to know and understand who God is because there will be a time when we lose our way and our missions. Strong knowledge of God's attributes steadies us and keeps us on track.

God does not change his promises. Once God commits, he keeps that commitment, and you can count on his character to keep his promises. You and I break a ton of promises in our lives. The power of the promise is not in the *words* of the promise but in the *character* of the one who makes it. God always keeps his promises because he is unchanging.

> *The power of the promise is not in the* words *of the promise but in the* character *of the one who makes it.*

> God is not a man, that he should lie, or a son of man, that he should change his mind. (Numbers 23:19 ESV)

I make promises, and even though I intend to keep them, I often do *not* keep those promises. I do this out of foolishness and out of a purely sinful, rebellious heart. God keeps his promises because he is not like us, but he did take on flesh and live among us. The gospel tells us that even though we have sinned, one who knew no sin would come and accomplish all the promises from the Father. This one is Jesus, and he is the King of all. Like Paul, let us believe in and stand on the truth:

> For all the promises of God find their Yes in him.
> (2 Corinthians 1:20 ESV)

The Communicable Attributes of God

I have highlighted that God is vastly different from his creation. He reigns on high and does need to identify with his creation to be who he is. In other words, God is God, no matter how he relates to his creation, and we can find a great deal of comfort in this truth. As a believer, I can rest in the assurance that God can go on without me; he doesn't need me. I also take a great deal of comfort in that truth. God, however, is not limited or defined merely by his incommunicable attributes.

Throughout the scriptures, we see evidence of how God is unlike us but also how we humans share some of his attributes. Theologians have named the attributes we share with the Creator as his communicable attributes. Some of these attributes are God's love, kindness, and patience.

Understanding God's communicable attributes helps the believer in two distinct ways. First, it's comforting to know that God is not only transcendent—meaning he transcends and is more significant than all things—but he is also imminent, or close at hand. Psalm 34:18 states that God is "near the brokenhearted." God is not only concerned with the state of his creation from afar, but he desires to be close to his creation no matter what is happening.

Second, understanding that God can experience some of the same emotions and experiences we do helps us understand the truth we find in Hebrews 4:15. The writer of Hebrews expresses God's communicable attributes with these words, concerning Jesus: "For we do not have a high priest who is unable to sympathize with our weaknesses, but one who has been tempted in every way as we are, yet without sin." There are powerful truths found in this verse. In Jesus, we have a God who understands what it means to be human. He understands the everyday experience a human goes through, and he has experienced all of our emotions and frailties in real time. He knows what it is like to love, hurt, and mourn. He understands what it is like to be misunderstood and despised. He also knows what it means to dine with friends and laugh with family.

He has experienced everything we encounter daily, and he sympathizes with us. What a great comfort it is to know that God has sympathy over us and our emotions today. Our feelings may be out of whack, but he understands and has compassion for us today. Not only does Jesus know the human experience all too well, but he also has lived this experience perfectly before the Father. Don't miss this: the writer of Hebrews expresses well the fact that even though Jesus lived among us, he never allowed sin to live in him. Our great King lived without sin and made way for his children to enter into the presence of the Father, clothed in his righteousness.

What does this mean for our emotions? It means our emotions can find a safe place in God. In Jesus, our feelings can be shaped and guided for his glory and his purpose. We are emotional people for a reason, and our emotions can bring glory to God.

> It means our emotions can find a safe place in God.

Questions for Personal Reflection

1. How are you ruled by your emotions, or the emotions of someone else, or your current circumstances?
2. In what ways are you comforted and encouraged to know that God is not like us?
3. Which attributes of God most stand out to you in this chapter?

CHAPTER 5
Gospel-Shaped Emotions

> For everything was created by him, in heaven and on earth, the visible and the invisible, whether thrones or dominions or rulers or authorities–all things have been created through him and for him. He is before all things, and by him all things hold together.
> —Colossians 1:16–17

My kids love art. They like to pull out scissors and glue and all kinds of different materials to bring life to their imaginations. Often I will enter their rooms to find their creations taped to the wall, telling the story of the free play they have just completed. They will make spy cameras and secret decoders they place on the outside of their doors.

I was never a fan of arts and crafts. I grew up going to Vacation Bible School, and I loved the games, the lessons, and especially the snacks, but I never wanted to do the crafts. Art was a requirement in high school, so to fulfill my credits to graduate, I enrolled in art during my sophomore year. We made a few projects and drew a couple of pictures, and for the most part, I felt confident in my artistic abilities.

Then we started a section on sculpting, and I saw how deficient my skills were. It all started with the potter's wheel. The assignment was simple. We had a choice to make one of four pieces of pottery: a coffee mug, an ashtray, a bowl, or a vase. My instructor informed the class that the bowl was the easiest to make, so I chose the bowl.

At first, it wasn't that difficult. I took the clay and made sure it was wet so it could be formed and manipulated into the form I desired. I took my seat at the potter's wheel and began the process of spinning the wheel and building the clay with my hands, hoping it would make the shape I desired.

It was a complete disaster! I tried every trick and tool my teacher gave me to form a bowl. I varied the speed of the wheel; I changed the tension and pressure I applied with my hands; I modified the amount of water I used—nothing worked. I started with a lump, and I finished with something that was somewhere in between a chunk of clay and a bowl. I was frustrated, irritated, and just plain angry with the entire process, but I could not give up because I needed a grade.

After a lot of work, my instructor looked at the creation in my hands and said, "That will have to do." I placed my work on a table marked with my name and hoped for a passing grade.

As I think back to that experience, I wonder what went wrong. Many of the other students made cups, bowls, and mugs that looked exquisite. One girl in my class made a teapot that was functional. I thought there must have been something wrong with the potter's wheel I used. I also thought my instructor didn't make sense, and if she could have explained the process better, then I wouldn't have been so embarrassed with what I made. You know, it wasn't the wheel's fault, or the tools I used, or the instruction I was given. The fault lay in my inability to mold the clay into the object I desired.

Many believers are in the same boat when it comes to their emotions. They have the tools, and they have heard sermons, developed techniques, and received counsel from professionals who have told them how to handle their feelings, yet their lives do not look the way they want after their emotions get out of control. I still remember watching the bowl I was trying to make as it started to take form. All of a sudden, a little wobble would develop, and I would apply low pressure in the wrong spot—and my creation once again resembled the lump I'd started with instead of the finished product I desired.

What goes wrong with our emotions often is the same thing that went wrong with my piece of pottery—it was in the wrong hands. If you were to take the same lump of clay, the same tools, and the same time spent and put all that in someone else's hands—someone who knows what he or she is doing—you would see that lump form into a piece of art.

We may allow circumstances, other people, or ourselves to shape our emotions when they need to be in the hand of the Master.

When Jesus saves us, he doesn't only protect us from our sins; he also saves us for a purpose. A believer's life should be guided and molded by the gospel every day. C. J. Mahaney refers to this process in his book, *A Christ-Centered Life*, as the ability to preach the gospel to yourself every day. Mahaney writes, "A cross-centered life is made up of cross-centered days."[1]

What does that mean? It means we allow the freshness of the gospel to order everything in our lives, and we are the ones calling ourselves to action in light of the gospel. Inward change happens because the effectiveness of the gospel is daily ordering our lives, and this not only changes our behaviors but our emotions as well.

A lot of preaching aims at behavior modification. Many have boiled down living a holy life into keeping themselves from a few things and answering the question of what their lives should not look like. Where this fails, however, is that the Bible calls our lives to look like something as well. The scriptures testify that our lives should look more like Jesus than ourselves. What does this mean for our emotions? It means our emotions should be shaped more by the gospel than by our attitudes, personalities, and present circumstances.

How Does the Gospel Shape Our Emotions?

People often associate the word *gospel* with phrases and ideas like "born again" or "being saved," yet the gospel is so much more. We do not experience the gospel only at the point of conversion but can and should experience the gospel every day of our lives. The term *gospel* means "good news." The good news of the birth, death, and resurrection of Jesus Christ has been the cornerstone of the Christian faith and the backbone of the church since its early days, but many today associate this beautiful word only with the moment of belief. In my opinion, many see the gospel just as an event, rather than the life-giving story that shapes and guides our stories. The gospel must not only save our lives; it must shape our lives as well.

The gospel is a message for every day, hour, and minute of our lives. This story can take the dull, seemingly unimportant events in our lives and turn them into moments that are defined by the glory of God.

> The gospel is a message for every day, hour, and minute of our lives.

Now, we must clarify some things. Is it true that once we hear and place our faith in Christ, it happens through the gospel? Absolutely! Paul wrote in Romans

10:8–9, "This is the message of faith that we proclaim: if you confess with your mouth, 'Jesus is Lord' and believe in your heart that God raised him from the dead, you will be saved." Did you catch that?

Paul wrote that we believe and confess Jesus as Lord as a result of the message of faith. What is this message of hope? It's the gospel, and it would be short-sighted not to affirm the fact that the nature of the gospel is evangelistic in every way. Conversion is only one face of the gospel. The gospel message shapes our discipleship and our growth as believers.

Everything in our lives is under the Lordship of Jesus, including our emotions. This statement does not mean Christians are dull, annoying, unemotional people. It does mean our feelings can find a safe place in the gospel of Jesus Christ. Discipleship happens when the people of God apply the word of God and the message of God to the everyday things that trigger their emotions. Our emotions often serve as an indicator of where the heart is. Jesus states, "For where your treasure is, there your heart will be also" (Matthew 6:21).

When my kids were little, they loved dressing up like pirates. My daughter had a "Pirate and Princess" party for her second birthday, and we didn't have to spend a lot of time convincing her and her friends to dress up. One of the games we played centered around finding a treasure and using a map. Jesus states that our hearts always will be where our treasures are, so find where your treasure is, and there you will find your heart.

> Everything in our lives is under the Lordship of Jesus, including our emotions.

How do you know what your treasure is? My daughter was like most two-year-olds; she needed help to find the treasure. She needed a guide, someone who was far greater and wiser than she was. We believers have one who is wiser and greater; we have Jesus. We have the Holy Spirit living inside of us, yet we often try to navigate life by ourselves. I often deceive myself when it comes to my holiness and spiritual health. I give myself far more credit than I should when it comes to what my heart truly desires. I will confuse my selfish anger with tough love. I will confuse the joy of the moment with the real pleasure that comes only from Christ.

I will say I am not anxious because Christians are strong and should not worry, but I should acknowledge my anxious thoughts and take them to the cross. I have allowed my emotions to shape me, instead of letting the gospel shape my emotions.

As the children of God, we can find our identities not in the culture or what is happening to us at the moment but in Jesus, our King. I believe the gospel of Jesus can shape our emotions so that everything we make points to his kingdom and his glory. This truth doesn't mean that our feelings will always obey the Spirit of the living God inside us, but it does say, "He who is in you, is greater than he who is in the world" (1 John 4:4 ESV). We Christians should not fear when our emotions seem out of control. We have a King who is more powerful than anything or anyone in the world. He sympathizes and understands our weaknesses and allows his children to come to him with all sorts of difficulties, even emotions that run amok and need restraining.

How does this happen? The process occurs when the authority and kingship of Jesus is applied to our minds, hearts, and, eventually, our actions. We don't have to check our emotions or leave our feelings at the door, but we do have to allow the gospel to shape how we experience life and see the world around us. As believers, once we enable the gospel to form our feelings, our emotions can point to the real treasure—Christ himself.

Questions for Personal Reflection

1. When are you most likely to take care of things and people with your own hands, rather than turning to Jesus?
2. Practically speaking, what does "preaching the gospel" to yourself daily look like?
3. Take time to survey your heart. What treasures do you find there? Which ones need to be discarded, taken to Jesus, and replaced with the treasure he provides?

CHAPTER 6
Why Am I So Angry?

> Summoning the crowd, he told them, "Listen and understand: It's not what goes into the mouth that defiles a person, but what comes out of the mouth—this defiles a person."
> —Matthew 15:11

I have often let anger get the best of me. Even as I type these words, I can recall many times when anger had control of my mind, heart, and actions, leading me down a road that I came to regret. I grew up in the shadow of an older brother—a brother who picked on me, especially in when I was in grade school. He is eight years my senior, an age gap that caused me to get on his nerves and that allowed him to do something about me when I did. Don't get me wrong; we had a great relationship growing up and have continued to have a great relationship as adults. Still, I can recall times when he made me mad—and by that, I don't mean he got under my skin or made me grumpy. I mean that he made me angry to the point of rage. But I take that back—my brother didn't make me angry; I was already angry. He just brought out what was bubbling inside.

I remember when that anger inside me came out with a vengeance. I was around ten years old, and my brother had a bunch of his friends over to swim in our pool. His friends treated me tremendously and always invited me to hang with them when they were over at our house. We played volleyball, jumped off the diving board, and enjoyed the summer sun. Then it happened: my brother placed me on his shoulders in the shallow end of the pool. That wasn't unusual—we played around in the pool all the time—but this time was different because after he hoisted me onto his shoulders, he started to get out of the pool. I asked him to stop, but he kept going—up the steps, around the rose bushes my dad had planted, and onto the diving board.

Despite my pleas, which had become rather loud at that point, he kept going until he reached the end of the diving board—and then he threw me in the water. I remember plummeting into the deep end of the pool. I could hear his friends' muffled reactions, and I could feel the sharp sting on my side where I had smacked the surface of the water. As I swam to the top of the water, the kind, likable little brother I'd been became a raving maniac. I don't know what I said, but it was directed at my brother and anyone who was associated with him. I believe I called him every name I could think of that would hurt his feelings and then told all his friends where they could go. I can still see some of his friends' faces as they realized that I had lost it.

I marched out of the pool, clutching my side and trying to hold back the tears. My brother asked me if I was all right, but I didn't want anything to do with him. I told him to leave me alone, and I ran into the kitchen, full of rage. I can still remember the feeling of wanting to attack him, to hurt him in some way, not so much physically but to retaliate.

He followed me into the kitchen, and I finally had my chance. I shouted at him, "I wish you had never come back from the hospital when you were a baby!" Now, those words don't seem that bad unless you have some family context—my brother had almost died as an infant. My parents would tell the story of how God saved him and preserved his life, showing that God was faithful to our family. My words meant something to both of us. I used them as a weapon against him. I wanted to hurt him, and I wanted him to feel the full fury of my rage.

Where did those words originate? How did a simple, playful act end in one brother telling another that he wished he never existed—wishing God had not intervened and saved him as a baby? What caused me to try to hurt my brother with words I had never thought to use against him before that day? Were those the words of a thoughtless brother? Was I just a stupid little guy whose his feelings were hurt? Was I foolishly enraged at that moment?

Paul Tripp states the following about foolish behavior: "Foolishness is more than being stupid, that deadly combination of arrogance and ignorance."[2] That day, the deadly combination of my anger, stupidity, and foolishness was a breeding ground for something deadly. My words came from my sinful nature, looking for an opening.

In Matthew 15, Jesus is very candid when he makes the statement that it is not what goes in people that defiles them but what comes out of them. Paul would write in Romans that sin was looking for an opportunity to seize control of these members. We all battle with sin and our old selves. My anger was looking for a chance to rear its ugly head and strike. Once I calmed down, I felt sorry and remorseful for the words I'd said. The only problem was that I'd said the words. They came out with emotion and fury. In my situation, it was not only the words I'd said but the way I said them—with an unsettled rage that resided deep within me controlling my tongue.

Have you ever snapped at someone? We use vernacular like the following to refer to anger: we "blow off steam," "lose our cool," or "erupt." Other expressions describe what we *feel* like when we are angry. Where do these emotions reside? Why can some of us go from a pleasant demeanor to a raging lunatic at the drop of a hat? I have seen people (myself included) take their anger out on a piece of equipment, or an animal, or even someone they love dearly. Many times, we lose our tempers with the ones we love the most.

One of the most critical aspects of understanding how to control our anger is to know where it originates. Many believe they are angry because an outside force or influence has affected them in some way. It may be the mail carrier who left your package in the rain; the neighbor who allows his animal to relieve himself every day on your front lawn; or the guy who cuts you off in traffic. The only problem with blaming an outside force is that it's nearly impossible to control every outside influence that affects your life.

Others believe anger is caused by the relationships they have—that if they limit their relationships with people who "push their buttons," then they can control their anger. People will use the silent treatment with others or limit their time around people they do not like. Again, this may work for a while, but what about when you are angry at a person you love? And what about believers who have sworn their allegiance to King Jesus and have placed their faith in him to follow in his words and teaching? Our Lord states in Matthew 5:43–44, "You have heard that it was said, Love your neighbor and hate your enemy. But I tell you, love your enemies and pray for those who persecute you."

For me, Jesus destroys my whole way of interacting with people. For the most part, I can love my neighbors or at least tolerate them, but love my enemies? I can't just separate myself from relationships as a way to control my anger. First, I have to acknowledge anger is flowing from inside my heart. Other situations, people, and circumstances only measure the anger in my heart. Do you remember how the gospel of John describes the night Jesus was arrested and betrayed? The account is in John 18:1–11, if you would like to read the scripture.

The chapter begins with Judas knowingly leading armed soldiers to the garden, where he knew Jesus and his disciples would be. John then gives us a little insight into the mind and heart of Jesus:

> Then Jesus, knowing everything that was about to happen to him, went out and said to them, "Who is it that you're seeking?" (John 18:4)

Think for a moment—if we knew what was going to happen, where would our emotions take us? I have to confess that if I knew what was about to happen to me—that I was about to be betrayed and handed over to men who would take my life—I wouldn't be as calm and collected as Jesus was. I would feel threatened, hurt, and, yes, angry. I would be like the man Simon Peter, who brought a sword to the garden. Jesus knew everything that would happen, but he had submitted his entire life to the will and purpose of the Father, so no outside influence would rattle or shake him. Jesus brought peace to the garden; Simon brought a sword—a sword he intended to use.

Our anger may be like Simon Peter's sword. That is, anger is something we carry around, deep inside, and we use it when we feel threatened or when we don't get our way. Just like Peter, we lash out with our anger when situations or threatening people come our way. We use anger to control a situation, or to put others in their places, or to shake our fists at the heavens because we feel let down or cheated in some way.

Why are we so angry? That's an excellent question. I still struggle to understand why anger gets the best of me. Jesus is more significant and grander than my anger. In this, I have hope.

The truth of this leads us to another question: is all anger terrible?

Questions for Personal Reflection

1. What makes you angry?
2. Do you struggle more with reacting in anger toward outside forces or people? Why?
3. Why was Jesus able to respond so differently than Peter when Judas betrayed him?

CHAPTER 7
When Can I Be Angry?

Be angry and do not sin. Don't let the sun go down on your anger, and don't give the devil an opportunity.
—Ephesians 4:26–27

God gave me an incredible opportunity to teach at a pastors' conference in Asia. My faith finds strength any time I have the chance to see what God is doing around the world, fulfilling the Great Commission through regular people who have given up their lives to follow Christ. The conference was designed to help local pastors mobilize their congregations to carry out the Great Commission and develop into active, healthy churches. The pastors I met were nothing short of astonishing. Many were bi-vocational and traveled far to hear four of us open the scriptures and train them for the ministry God called them to accomplish.

During one of the sessions, a fellow pastor asked the group to consider this thought: "Does your heart break for the things that break the heart of God?" This statement is simple yet profound, and it's an excellent question to ask regarding where our hearts are oriented when it comes to anger.

The word *anger* carries a specific negative connotation. At first glance, it seems to be something we should suppress or even rid our lives of completely. If I could promise you a life where you were never angry at anyone or any situation, you might take it. To live without losing your cool is a pretty good option. Now, let's look at the other side. Are there times when anger is the appropriate emotion in a particular situation? Are there times when we look at a world that is plagued with sin and hurt, with heartache and abuse, violence and evil, and we feel that anger is the appropriate response? The problem I see is that we don't know *why* we are angry, and therefore, anger controls us instead of our expressing anger appropriately. Ultimately, we are often angry at the wrong things.

Think for a moment about what makes you angry. Your boss, your kids, cold coffee, missed deadlines—they all have one thing in common. Someone has offended you or broken your laws. I have to confess that most of my anger has nothing to do with evil in the world or the oppression of the poor or hurt. My anger mostly centers on people and circumstances that make my life uncomfortable. Many times, the anger in my life is unwarranted, and because I have no real reason to be angry, I often get lost in my anger. Have you ever found yourself angry, upset, or frustrated—and suddenly you snap? You may express yourself with words, a gesture, or a look. Then time passes, you calm down, and you think, *Why was I even angry?* Again, I think many believers don't know what they are angry about, let alone if we have a right to be angry. Many Christians live their lives with a mob mentality with regard to their anger. They follow the crowd in what makes them angry.

> Ultimately, we are often angry at the wrong things.

I am more like the world than I am unlike the world, which I hate to admit. The things that often make me angry are when my creature comforts are not there. Take away my happiness, and you will see me throw a tantrum. Mess with my agenda, and I will act like a two-year-old who was not allowed an ice cream before dinner. An excellent question to ask at this point is this: *when* should I be angry? I believe if we knew *when* anger is the best emotion to express, our lives wouldn't be ruled by anger as much. We need to let the gospel shape our anger. To state it another way, the heart of God should drive our anger.

Be Angry, and Do Not Sin

My hostile attitude has often led me down paths I wished I had never traveled. You may be in the same boat. We can do a lot of damage in a little amount of time when our anger is out of control, but there is a better way: we can let the gospel shape our anger. You can be an angry person without being a sinful, angry person. A lot of the decisions we make while angry tend to end in an immoral action or behavior. Paul is clear when he states, "Be angry and do not sin. Don't let the sun go down on your anger, and don't give the devil opportunity" (Ephesians 4:26–27), but believers do not always heed Paul's words when they are angered.

Look at the text; Paul instructs the church in Ephesus to "be angry and do not sin." Paul is saying there are times when it is right and good to be angry. The actions of our Lord show us it's actually just to be angry, such as when he saw the corruption of the gouging of prices and quality of the sacrifices sold in the court of the Gentiles of the temple in John 2:13–17. He turned over their tables and drove them out with a whip he had fashioned with cords. Jesus often saw the corruption and the hard-heartedness of the religious leaders of his day.

> We can do a lot of damage in a little amount of time when our anger is out of control, but there is a better way: we can let the gospel shape our anger.

In the book of Mark, Jesus asked the leaders of Israel a question about healing a man with a withered hand on the Sabbath. The response of the leaders was silence. After looking around at them with anger, he was grieved at the hardness of their hearts and told the man, "Stretch out your hand." So he stretched it out, and his hand was restored. (Mark 3:5)

God is described in the Old Testament as one who is "slow to anger and abounding in faithful love" (Psalm 103:8). God is not just a God of love but of justice and divine wrath, yet it is clear from scripture that he is slow to anger and gracious to all. Followers of Christ can express themselves with anger when anger is justified, and this does not cause sin. Take a moment to evaluate what makes you angry, and ask yourself an important question: *Do the same things that anger the heart of God anger my heart as well?* Brother and sister, this helps us in our battle against sinful anger and out-of-control emotions.

Paul also instructs believers not to let the sun go down on their anger. The instruction means there is a time limit to our anger. We can't be angry all the time, even when it is justified. Some people seem to be looking for a fight these days. They are offended and angry with everything and everyone who dares oppose their views of the world or their way of thinking. It's an understatement to say they have a chip on their shoulders. Paul understood there are times to be angry, but he clarifies this by giving a time restraint on anger.

Jesus said in Matthew 5:9, "Blessed are the peacemakers, for they will be called the sons of God." Paul wrote in Romans 12:18, "If possible, as far as it depends on you, live at peace with everyone." One of the best habits to practice in our Christian lives is overlooking an offense. There are times when anger is the right response, but even when we are angry, we must sort through our anger and offer on-the-spot forgiveness. By this, I mean offering forgiveness by overlooking the offense in that moment. I believe if we were more keenly aware of our own need for forgiveness, our own need for grace, our own need for redemption, and the depth of our sins, then we would not hold on to our anger, even if we were justified in it.

Finally, Paul says we should not "give the devil an opportunity." Other translations say not to give the devil a "foothold." Jesus described the devil with these words: "A thief comes only to steal and kill and destroy" (John 10:10).

As Peter instructs the church, "Be sober-minded, be alert. Your adversary, the devil, is prowling around like a roaring lion, looking for anyone he can devour" (1 Peter 5:8). The devil is looking for an opportunity to strike, and when he gets his shot at a believer, he will strike.

A good example of a *foothold* would be a stirrup on a saddle. A rider uses a stirrup to mount a horse and sit in the saddle. The devil is prowling around, seeing who he may devour. He is a selective hunter who looks for those who are not strong in the Spirit and are weak in the flesh. Once he sees an opportunity, he looks to devour and destroy. How do we prevent giving the devil an opportunity? Peter's answer is in the first sentence of 1 Peter 5:8; he says a believer should be "sober-minded."

You can't be sober-minded and drunk with anger at the same time.

Anger may take a wrong turn when we refuse to live by the Spirit, and we embrace living by the flesh. My flesh is weak, and your flesh is weak, but his Spirit is powerful. When we chose to live by the Spirit, we say yes to Jesus's instruction and no to our sinful desires. So be angry, but be angry at the right things. The only way to do this is by living in and through the Spirit.

> You can't be sober-minded and drunk with anger at the same time.

Questions for Personal Reflection

1. What are examples of acceptable anger (that which angers God) and unacceptable anger (that which is born from sin)? How do we express each?
2. How can you change from being self-minded to sober-minded?
3. How is God challenging you to live by the Spirit of God and the truth of his Word?

CHAPTER 8
How the Gospel Shapes Our Anger

Truly I tell you, wherever this gospel is proclaimed in the whole world, what she has done will also be told in memory of her.
—Matthew 26:13

Sometimes we need perspective in life, and fortunately, the gospel offers the attitude we need. The gospel redirects and reorients our lives so we can see, with clarity, the ultimate plan of God. Fundamentally, the gospel shapes our lives. The gospel can also develop our emotional well-being. Our emotions are important and can bring glory and honor to the King, or they can highlight our sinfulness.

Matthew records Jesus's anointing at Bethany in chapter 26 of his gospel. Jesus found himself in the home of Simon, the leper. First of all, no Jewish man, especially a teacher, would defile himself by eating at the home of a leper. While eating and reclining at the table, a woman entered and poured an expensive bottle of perfume on Jesus's head. Most agree this perfume would cost somewhere between $30,000 and $35,000 by today's standards. The perfume was probably a family heirloom or an extraordinary mixture used to ready a vital family member for burial.

> The gospel redirects and reorients our lives so we can see, with clarity, the ultimate plan of God.

The gospel of Matthew records two different perspectives regarding this event—the disciples' and Jesus's. The disciples had an emotional reaction to it. Matthew 26:8 says this about their response:

> When the disciples saw it, they were indignant, "Why this waste?" they asked. The disciples see the action as a waste

and became angry; verse 9 states, "For this could have been sold for a large sum and given to the poor" (ESV).

As I've mentioned, it's right to be angry when we see foolish behavior. I would have agreed with the disciples, if not for Jesus's words in the passage. Verse 10 states the following, "But Jesus, aware of this, said to them, 'Why do you trouble the woman? For she has done a beautiful thing to me" (ESV). Maybe you would have agreed with the disciples too, or maybe our hearts would have been moved by the Spirit to accept the words of Jesus and too see the act as something beautiful.

Many times we react to life by being in the moment. In-the-moment decisions help us to justify our actions and our emotions. The disciples justified their emotions when they saw the act as a waste. Their perception, worldview, and reasoning led to their emotions. Their emotions were shaped by what they saw in the temporal; Jesus wanted them to focus on the eternal.

My emotions tend to ebb and flow because they are reacting to what I see happening on the temporal plane before me. I do not have the eternal perspective I need, so anything that sets my emotions off—big or small, important or unimportant—tends to control my reactions. The disciples' reactions shaped their emotions, instead of the gospel and the words of Jesus forming their emotions.

> Their emotions were shaped by what they saw in the temporal; Jesus wanted them to focus on the eternal.

You may ask, *Do my emotions shape my decisions, or do my decisions shape my emotions?* Both may be true. When our emotions are not under the control of the Spirit, we may make hasty decisions, allowing our emotions to control our decisions. When we make unwise choices that are contrary to God's law, then we find ourselves in difficult circumstances, and these circumstances can lead to out-of-control emotions. In both instances, the gospel needs to shape our decisions and emotions.

Listening to the Master

When God speaks, we need to listen. When God speaks, our emotions should bow down and react appropriately to his words. There is no room for angry disciples in the presence of a peaceful and calm Lord. Let's remind ourselves of the reaction of Jesus in Matthew 26:10:

> Aware of this, Jesus said to them, "Why are you bothering this woman?"

> There is no room for angry disciples in the presence of a peaceful and calm Lord.

Jesus doesn't rebuke his disciples, nor does he agree with their assessment of the situation at hand. Jesus's emotions do not match the emotions of his disciples. Here, we see the same situation but a different emotional response. Jesus questions their response and then frames their answer with the gospel.

The disciples validate their response by pointing out the poor handling of the situation by the woman. The perfume could have served a better cause; the cause brought forth was caring for the poor, but truthfully, it could have been any noble cause, like caring for widows, children, or any other obligation a believer has to humanity. Watch how this passage unfolds and observe how Jesus reframes their response.

Matthew 26:11–12 continues: "You always have the poor with you, but you do not always have me. By pouring this perfume on my body, she has prepared me for burial." Jesus informs his disciples of an important truth; if we don't see life through the lens of the gospel, then we do not see life correctly. The disciples make the situation about solving a problem. Jesus makes it about himself; namely, his death, burial, and resurrection, which is the gospel message.

Jesus's reaction takes the disciples from a temporal view of life and elevates their view to an eternal perspective. The psalmist would write these words: "Who do I have in heaven but you? And I desire nothing on earth but you. My flesh and heart may fail, but God is the strength of my heart, my portion forever" (Psalm 73:25–26). Note the importance of the words of this psalm. Because of the realization of the power and glory of God, the psalmist understands there is nothing on earth that compares to the glory of God. Even if our lives and hearts fail, he is our portion forever. This kind of worldview allows us to live with an eternal perspective, and Jesus is directing the disciples to regard the actions of the women not as a waste but as an appropriate response to perform in the presence of the King of kings.

The gospel is primary; caring for the poor is secondary. Caring for the poor, correctly and justly, flows from a heart that understands the relevance and power of the gospel. When the gospel shapes our emotions, they pay attention, just a like a good soldier who follows orders from the commander. There is a rank and file in the military, and so it is with our emotions. The gospel of Christ commands our emotions to stop and act accordingly. One of the problems with anger is in the way reactions are made at the moment. Those of us who struggle with anger may allow our feelings to dictate our actions at a moment's notice. We see something we disagree with, and we react. We may not have the spiritual maturity to access a situation and see the larger picture.

The disciples were angry because they were living in the moment and could not see the bigger picture. Anger has a way of blocking our views of the bigger picture. When anger takes control, rational, thoughtful decisions give way to fast, irrational ones. The disciples were quick to speak and slow to hear. This humble woman, however, acted accordingly by giving something precious to the King.

The disciples attached themselves to their anger, while the woman was attached to the gospel. What does Jesus say about this? "Truly I tell you, wherever this gospel is proclaimed in the whole world, what she has done will also be told in memory of her" (Matthew 26:13). In this life and in the next, Jesus is the final and ultimate authority, and he will have the last word. Our anger and our fickle emotions will not have the final say; the Son of God will utter the final words.

Questions for Personal Reflection

1. With which perspective in Matthew 26 do you most identify? Why?
2. How will you respond to God's eternal perspective and that Jesus is the final and ultimate authority?
3. How have you become an angry disciple? Confess these areas to God, and ask him to give you his perspective.

CHAPTER 9
Slowing Down Our Anger

> My dear brothers and sisters, understand this: Everyone
> should be quick to listen, slow to speak, and slow to anger.
> —James 1:19

I hope that by this point, we, as believers, can see that our anger can get the best of us, and the gospel should shape our anger, rather than our having in-the-moment reactionary outbursts. How does this work in practicality? How do we put our anger on a leash and allow it not to control so many of our reactions? I won't give you a step-by-step process, but I'll make practical observations from the book of James that can be very beneficial.

Everyone, Listen Up

It's important to be self-aware of how you behave and how others view your behavior. Understanding yourself and how you interact with people around you is critical, not only for life but for the Christian life we have with Christ. James appeals to his faith family to understand a couple of key concepts with regard to their behavior. Understanding is crucial to spiritual change. *The change will never happen if you never recognize the need for change to occur.* I see dear brothers and sisters struggle with comprehension. We are living in a very reactionary age. People tend to get offended very quickly, and their emotions respond to how they get hurt. We are so busy being offended that we fail to understand our role in the offense.

> The change will never happen if you never recognize the need for change to occur.

When Christ directs your life, you gain wisdom

and understanding. The book of Proverbs is full of verses that instruct us to understand and seek knowledge. Proverbs 2:2 states, "listening closely to wisdom and directing your heart to understanding." In Proverbs 2:11, we read, "Discretion will watch over you, and understanding will guard you." A correct understanding of yourself often leads to a proper understanding of the situation you are facing.

We tend to bring little or no knowledge of a situation or of someone's words or actions, which allows small room for discretion. When we understand what is going on with us, God, and whatever we are facing, we have a better chance of controlling our emotions.

James wants his readers to understand three things. First, we are to listen. I am not a good listener, but I want to be. Maybe you identify with this. I am often guilty of acting like I'm listening when I am just preparing, in my mind, what I am about to say in rebuttal to what I *think* I have heard (but I wasn't listening). Communication is so important in relationships, and the ability to communicate is paramount. Communication is not just the transfer of ideas and words; it's the ability to understand what is said. I often know I have communicated something very clearly, but it wasn't received because the person to whom I was speaking was not listening.

Hearing and listening are not the same things. I hear things all the time; it doesn't mean I can tell you the motive or the intention of the words I hear. James is saying to his readers to be quick to listen. When we are ready to listen, we allow our mind to think through the situation which slows the emotional response of anger. Anger is often fast, and we have to slow it down. Listening helps us to keep control of our anger and not let it get the best of us.

Practice active listening. This involves listening in such a way that we hear *and* understand what the person is saying. Don't just listen with your ears; allow your mind and body to engage in the conversation. We all have to partake in crucial conversations—conversations that need to be held but that can escalate quickly. These conversations may be tense at times, and it's important to clarify what is said. Try to repeat what you have heard from an individual. This technique helps to explain communication between individuals. When I slow down and ask others what they meant by a word, remark, or comment, it gives them an opportunity for further explanation and a better chance for me to listen.

Don't rush to blow up at your kids; listen first. Don't rush to conclusions with your spouse; listen first. Dear brothers and sisters, give one another grace and the benefit of the doubt, and hear well.

Not Every Thought Should Be Expressed

James continues his line of thinking in calling believers to be slow to speak. It's tough to take words back. The book of Proverbs says, "When there are many words, sin is unavoidable, but the one who controls his lips is prudent" (Proverbs 10:19). Words are easy to say, but appropriate, good words are often hard to find. I have been around people who have no problem with speaking their minds. I have known a lot of people who like to advertise their ability to speak their minds, but just because you like to speak your mind doesn't mean you should do so. As believers, we should live and speak with discretion and care.

Speaking exact words is a spiritual discipline. James spoke earlier in his writing about the power of the tongue and words. Believers should take seriously the words written in James 3:9, which tells us, "With the tongue, we bless our Lord and Father, and with it we curse people who are made in God's likeness." Our words can be a blessing or a curse. Often, it's not the words themselves that get us into trouble; it's the tone and emotion behind the words.

In my marriage, I may have a harsh tone and an attitude behind my words. My harsh tone often happens when I have not slowed down to think before I speak. Anger will grab the steering wheel of my heart, and out of my mouth flow words drenched in deep-rooted anger. Again, Proverbs gives validity to the power of our words.

> The tongue of the wise makes knowledge attractive, but
> the mouth of fools blurts out foolishness. (Proverbs 15:2)

When we pause to listen, think, and then respond, we have a much better chance to bring glory and honor to God with our words and to control the anger that may be lurking. Measure your words, take the time to think before you speak, and even pray before you speak. Be quick to listen and slow to speak—but James doesn't stop there.

Kevin Wilson

Turning from Anger

Once we have listened well and measured our response to what we have heard, then we can respond with the correct emotion. Remember, sometimes anger is the proper response to a situation, but the emotion of anger should be controlled by the Holy Spirit of God, since we, as believers, are children of God. Anger should not always be the response when we disagree or feel threatened by another person. A person may not begin with the emotion of anger. His or her anger elevates as he or she feels threatened by the opposing force—the other person.

Our anger passes through stages, like the pain index medical professionals use to determine how much pain you are experiencing. We may start at a one on the anger index, but after a few texts or interactions on social media, we are quickly at a seven. We may begin a conversation with our children that is calm and peaceful, but after a few exchanges, we go from a one to a nine on the anger index. The day-to-day grind of a relationship often brings a person who is calm and cool to the point of exploding with anger. That's the challenge when it comes to anger; this emotion escalates quickly. We don't have a lot of reaction time.

James is clearly saying to slow down. Be quick to listen, slow to speak, and slow to anger. This leads us to a question: how do you stay calm when the other person is losing it? A lot of people find themselves triggered into an angry outburst by another's outburst of anger.

> He also told them a parable: "Can the blind guide the blind? Won't they both fall in a pit?" (Luke 6:39)

These are good words to apply when we find ourselves in the middle of a conversation that's verging on an emotional meltdown. We often get caught up in someone else's blind rage and end up falling into the same pit in which they have fallen.

As a believer, you don't have to give in to your anger or even to the anger of another person. Anger may be misused; that is, it's not the right emotion to use in a conversation or situation. Think of your emotions as different tools in a toolbox. An expert carpenter knows how to access the situation and grab the right tool for the job. The right tool makes all the difference. You don't use a saw when a hammer is needed, nor do you use a set of pliers when a drill is needed. A lot of times we use anger when compassion is needed. We reach for anger when love is needed. When someone else uses the wrong emotion, you don't need to follow suit.

I am trying to practice what I preach. When threatened and provoked by others, our response is critical to keeping our anger under control. Proverbs 15:1 is a verse my family has memorized and put to use as we interact with one another: "A gentle answer turns away anger, but a harsh word stirs up wrath." Our response to someone else's anger will either help or hurt that person's walk with the Lord. As believers, our answer to the anger of others should be one of peace and gentleness. As believers, we should be more like fire extinguishers instead of fire-starters. Sometimes a gentle answer is the difference between sin and obedience.

Questions for Personal Reflection

1. Who/what do you have the hardest time tolerating?
2. How does listening vs. hearing help slow down your anger?
3. What step do you need to take to bring your conversations into obedience with James 1:19?

CHAPTER 10
Understanding the Righteousness of God

For human anger does not accomplish God's righteousness.
—James 1:20

A lot of our anger tries to bring a solution to something we find unacceptable. For instance, someone cuts in front of us in traffic, and we see this as unacceptable, so we lash out in anger. The tension and frustration that fellow drivers have with one another has been given its own vernacular. We call it *road rage*. A lot of times we use anger to correct what we feel is unjust. Someone breaks a command or crosses a boundary, and in our anger, we attempt to set things right. There are a couple of problems with this approach. First, we generally are the one seeing the law, commands, and boundaries. As mentioned earlier, we are most offended and angered when someone messes with our way of looking at the world. We may act like judge, jury, and executioner when it comes to those who break our standards and rules, but many times, the people we target with our anger don't know they have broken the laws of our little kingdoms.

Second, we often use our anger to punish and correct those who have transgressed against us. We use anger to bring people to justice. It may be a piercing glare at the guy who answers his phone in the movie theater, or a good tongue-lashing to the waiter who miscalculated our tab. You can count on this fact: whatever form your anger takes, it is because someone has offended you and your own set of laws.

Sometimes we are angry for the right reasons—our anger lines up with God's anger. We see the way God sees, and we respond to a situation with the appropriate anger response. Just because we are angry at the right things, however, does not mean we are using anger in the right way.

Anger can be a way of putting things right in a world gone wrong, but if we are not careful and humble, especially with our words, we will do more harm than good. In his letter to the early church, James has essential things to say to believers on the motivation behind anger.

> Just because we are angry at the right things, however, does not mean we are using anger in the right way.

As stated before, we should be slow to anger. We should pick our emotions carefully and with wisdom, not letting them have the steering wheels of our hearts and souls. A lot of times we use anger as an attempt to bring justice to a situation with which we disagree. For example, our kids misbehave, and we lose our cool. Sometimes anger becomes a tool we use to shape the behavior we want to see in our kids. Many well-meaning parents, including me, use misplaced anger to correct our children; we believe anger can motivate our children to do and be good.

As parents, we may think that our anger will produce a change in our children. First of all, we can't change anyone, even our children. We can influence people's decisions, but ultimately, God is the only one who can turn a heart. Second, anger usually is not the best tool to teach someone a lesson, especially out-of-control anger. James shows an important truth to keep before us when it comes to our anger; namely, our anger does not produce the righteousness of God.

James penned the following: "For human anger does not accomplish God's righteousness" (James 1:20). James's desire was for God's people to know that their anger would not produce the one thing they desperately needed from a holy God—his righteousness.

The Righteousness of God

How do we receive the righteousness of God? Do we need the righteousness of God, or can we, by sheer human merit, gain the righteousness of God?

When we try to bring about the righteousness of God through human endeavor, we counteract the grace of God that saves us. The gospel has *nothing* to do with human effort or human cunning. My anger often is not a result of something that has happened to me; instead, I use my anger to get something I want to happen. I am not saying we should not be advocates for right living or righteousness, in general. I am saying that our righteousness and the righteous actions we want to see in other situations is ushered in by the living God of the Bible. When we take matters in our own hands, we usually go astray. Why? Because we do not know what we want. We are blinded and misled by our own emotions and behaviors.

Let's use parenting as an example where anger is used in the wrong way to form the right actions and behaviors. You may not be a parent, but I find myself in the days of parenting young kids, and it's the one place where I see God stretching and growing me now. I want to train and instruct my son and daughter well. I want to see them grow up to love the God I love and to embrace the convictions I hold dear. The desire drives and motivates me in many ways, and too often, I will take things into my own hands in the shaping of their little hearts and minds.

> My anger often is not a result of something that has happened to me; instead, I use my anger to get something I want to happen.

Aren't parents supposed to be active and involved in their kids' lives, shaping their thoughts, hearts, and minds? Of course! The problem is not the principles we teach; it's the way we go about teaching and training.

A believing parent has many tools to use. We have an example. We show our children how to live; we teach them how to conduct themselves with others. We teach them patience, hoping our model will be a beacon during the night, helping them to navigate the human experience without crashing into the rocky shores of life. We have the scriptures.

> All Scripture is inspired by God and is profitable for teaching, for rebuking, for correcting, and training in righteousness. (2 Timothy 3:16)

God has given parents his word to help their children strengthen their faith and align their beliefs with the God of the universe. Often we do not use these good tools that God has given. Instead, we choose to use our anger as the primary tool to influence the behavior of our children. I am not saying our children will never make us angry, but our anger never accomplishes what the cross of Jesus can. Our children need to show respect, and "training in righteousness" is a very important task for any believing parent, yet our anger at our kids' disobedience never produces the righteousness of God. For generations, parents and believers have tried to pound the faith into the next generation instead of training the next generation in what it means to follow Christ. Scores of people have been turned off to the faith by well-meaning but misguided followers of Jesus. We must keep our anger under control as we interact with others.

This message is not just for parents. This message is helpful as we communicate with our coworkers and those on social media and in the everyday interactions we have each day. We want to see many experience the life-changing work of the Holy Spirit, as the gospel is heard and believed. We want to see people radically changed in their hearts, their minds, and their behaviors, but increasing the volume on our anger will never produce the righteousness of God in the lives of others.

I think a classic mistake made by many believers, including me, is that our anger and disgust with sin can change the lives of others, making them righteous before God. As I've mentioned, the gospel has *nothing* to do with our endeavors. I don't mean that our faith is without tangible works. Faith without works is dead, but our behavior does not change because someone has made us feel guilty about our actions or attitudes. Real change occurs because Jesus has changed us. Our anger can never produce the righteousness God desires in the life of a believer.

How have you tried to spread the message of the gospel? Is it through long-suffering and graciousness or angry rhetoric? I don't want to harp on the use of social media these days, but it amazes me how often I see believers attack the world, culture, and each other with hateful words laced with bitterness, instead of gracious speech seasoned with salt.

Take a moment. Are you using your anger to try to do something only the gospel of Christ can do? We all fall into this trap, using our anger to accomplish the work of God, but it doesn't have to be this way. The church has been rescued by one who took the full wrath of God on the cross. Jesus graciously sacrificed himself for our salvation. We can't shake our fists at the world and embrace the cross at the same time. It's okay to be angry and disgusted with sin and its effect on the world around us, but being angry all the time will never accomplish the plan of God.

Questions for Personal Reflection

1. When has your anger been revealed because of feelings of inadequacy, insecurity, and deficiency?
2. Reflect on your own experience with God. What drew you into a relationship with Jesus? Was it a recognition of your sin, his grace, or a combination of both?
3. After removing all circumstances and excuses, with whom are you angry? Is it you? Is it God?

CHAPTER 11
The Weight of Anxiety

Anxiety in a person's heart weighs it down,
but a good word cheers it up.
—Proverbs 12:25

My wife and I purchased our first house outside of Charlotte, North Carolina, in 2008. We watched as the builders poured the foundation and added the walls, and we watched our dreams become a reality as the keys to our new home were handed over to us. After all the waiting, it was time to move in; the house was ours. I can remember decorating our house for Halloween and waiting by the door, anticipating our first trick-or-treaters. I can remember the smell of the candles Kristina purchased so our home would give off a pleasant aroma to those who entered our little habitat. I always felt safe when I was home. We had an alarm system installed and a sign outside that warned intruders to stay away because this house was under surveillance and protection. We both worked, so we would lock the doors and go our separate ways to accomplish the work God provided for us. Thinking back, it was an enjoyable time, but not every day was enjoyable.

I came home early one day, right before the Christmas holiday. When I arrived, I noticed the front door was ajar. I pulled into the driveway, and as I made my way to the front door, I found it had been kicked in, and our Christmas wreath, which we had hung with great care, lay in the middle of the hallway. I thought, *What is going on?* Thankfully, I had the presence of mind to call the local authorities so they could make sure no one was in the house at the time.

Then I called Kristina and told her, "Don't panic, but our house has been broken into." I never thought I would call to tell her those words. I always thought my house was safe and secure, protected by signs, locks, and alarms. We found out from the authorities that thieves had broken into several homes that day using the same technique. They would find a house built with alcove for a front porch. This design allowed them to be hidden from view while they broke into the home. Their plan was to kick in the door, run to the nearest room, and make off with whatever they could take. The thieves made off with a lot of valuables from our neighbors, but what they stole from our house was personal. They took my wife's wooden jewelry box, which had a necklace her grandmother had given her. The peace we once enjoyed each night as we slept was now interrupted by the events of the day.

Our hearts were anxious and heavy for many days. We lived with an uncertainty while in our house. Things didn't seem right; the security we once felt was replaced with the memory of being robbed. I think this is what anxiety in our hearts often does. Worry robs us from savoring and enjoying the life God has given us to live. On more than one occasion, I have gone to sleep worried about something, only to be assaulted by the same worry and anxiety seconds after I awake the following day.

Anxiety comes in all forms. We find big things to worry about; we see little things to worry over. We make small things into big things and worry about them. We worry and fret over people, places, and situations. We worry about the past, the present, and, indeed, the future. We worry about our money; we worry about our marriages; we worry and fret over who we are going to marry and even if we will find that special someone. We worry over kids—man, I never knew how much I feared until I had kids. I worry about them crossing the street, meeting a stranger, getting injured, getting lost.

I have to be honest; writing this section alone has caused a bit of anxiety in me. Some of us have anxiety that alters our quality of life. If this describes you, then seeing a trained licensed professional is a wise decision. Anxiety is nothing to dismiss or to not take seriously. It will rob you of joy and happiness and will cause you to take your eyes off Jesus and his great love for you.

I can testify that anxiety has stolen a lot of time and energy from my life. I have spent hours worrying and have not seen any forward movement in my life because of what I was experiencing and feeling. Anxiety often makes a person feel hopeless. Anxious people will often feel insecure and out of control, isolating themselves from people and a God who loves them. Proverbs 12:25 states that a troubled heart is heavy, burdened by the circumstances of the world. It's heavy with fear and worry, and often these emotions take over our day; we take our eyes off the everyday moments of grace given by a loving Lord. Worry often steals more than we'd like to admit.

> Worry often steals more than we'd like to admit.

Let's examine three ways worry can rob you blind.

Anxiety Steals the Security We Find in Christ

Worry and fear have a way to make us doubt the security we find in Christ. The world is always trying to define our identity. The world wants to conform us to its set pattern. Every age has attempted to rewire the DNA of the children of God. The enemy knows if he can make you doubt who you are in Christ, then he can attack the weakness you have in your fleshly body. Jesus says these words to his sleepy disciples on the night of his betrayal: "Stay awake and pray, so that you won't enter into temptation. The spirit is willing, but the flesh is weak" (Matthew 26:41).

Anxiety can weaken our flesh, and we find our spirits are not strong enough to fight off the things we fear and fret over. Anxiety wants to conquer us. Worry intends to strip away the peace we experience in Christ by abiding in his presence. The enemy knows this one thing about someone who is a believer. Once we lose our security, anxiety takes over like a virus, unleashing thoughts and fears we thought we would never experience.

Anxiety Steals Our Hope for the Future

Anxiety wages war against the hope the believer has in the future. A Christian worldview paints a very positive and encouraging future. As believers, we know certain truths that drive the hope we have. We understand this world is not all there is. Our future is not tied up in the present life. We know we have a future home in heaven with God the Father and his Son, Jesus Christ, who has made way for us by the provision of his death, burial, and resurrection.

> In him you also were sealed with the promised Holy Spirit when you heard the word of truth, the gospel of salvation, and when you believed. The Holy Spirit is the down payment of our inheritance, until the redemption of the possession, to the praise of his glory. (Ephesians 1:13-14)

Paul informs the church that God has secured their future by way of the down payment of the Holy Spirit. God now possesses his children by his indwelling Spirit, giving them victory over sin and preparing them for the glory, to be revealed in the heavenly places. We remind ourselves of these truths as we journey through life, looking forward to the inheritance we have in Christ. Anxiety tends to cast a shadow on the theological truths of the scriptures. God says our future is secure, but worry makes us question our future. God says he loves us so much that he is preparing a place for our future, but anxiety makes us wonder if his love is secure and eternal. God says that nothing will be able to separate us from the love that is found in Jesus Christ. Worry makes us question every decision we have made and reminds us of all the obstacles and obstructions that seem to hide the delight of his presence from us. God wants our faith to be secure in his presence, his Word, and his power. Worry has a way of deflating our hopes and hiding the reality of God's existence and presence in our daily experiences.

Anxiety Steals the Joy of Abiding in Christ

Worry and fear have a way of ruining the joy we find in Christ in our everyday experience. Most of the pleasure we experience in the Christian life is not seen in the mountaintop experiences but in the everyday situations of life. Like Elijah in 1 Kings 18, we experience the joy and triumph of the Lord on the mountain, only to see ourselves running, scared, alone, and seemingly abandoned by God. Anxiety and fear can creep in and rob us of the joy of the abiding presence of Christ when we focus on what is happening to us externally, instead of what Jesus is doing in us internally.

Worry often becomes the operating system we use to process life. We see the events unfolding around us—not through the sovereign reign of God but through our ability to handle the situation. We have to deal with a truth

Gospel Shaped Emotions

that unsettles us to the core. The fact is, we can't handle most situations. It may seem we are in control; it may seem we have everything worked out. It may seem we have a solution to every problem that can happen and an answer to every question that may come up.

Worry and fear, however, paint another picture; it's the portrait of what-if. What if I missed a detail? What if I face a situation that doesn't make sense? What if the answer I thought was right is wrong? What if my faith fails? What if my flesh fails? What if I am not strong enough, smart enough, or talented enough? Anxiety, fear, and worry can turn every circumstance on its head and leave us afraid and alone, isolated from others and isolated from a God who loves us so. We all live with this tension in our lives. What if I fail? What if God fails? Anxiety will pounce on us and have no mercy.

Not long ago, I was very anxious about a circumstance, and I wrote these words as a prayer to the Father in my journal: "Father, I felt my anxiety creep up on me like an army advancing on a wall." That's how worry made me feel. Instead of my being met by the joy of the Lord in the morning, I would begin the day with fear because of what I felt the day might bring. We question our existences and his love for us, but we need to hear and believe what God says about our identities when worry has robbed us. Proverbs 12:25 lets us know we need to listen to a cheerful word.

The Gospel Restores What Anxiety Takes

Proverbs 12:25 lets us know the feeling anxiety brings is not the final word. Worry can easily make us feel heavy and burdened by the weight of life. The emotions that anxiety brings will often try to shape our identities and the purposes we have. Too often, I have allowed the things I worry about to control and dictate how I act and respond during my day. Fear and worry will make me blow things out of proportion, making the challenges I face bigger, scarier, and darker than they are. In my life, I have allowed anxiety to speak louder and more clearly than the one who created me and knew me intimately. Our lives get out of order when anything speaks louder than the voice of our Father.

> Our lives get out of order when anything speaks louder than the voice of our Father.

At just the right time, the cross of Jesus rescues us and brings a message of good news; this is the answer we need! The gospel is more than an event; it's a message, and this message can shape our lives and order our days better than worry or fear. When we view our lives through the lenses of anxiety, we see chaos; even the things that seem in order can look chaotic. Worry is like a funhouse mirror that distorts reality intentionally, and so does anxiety and fear. Worry can make us stressed out about things we know deep in our hearts are not true. When anxiety amps us up, it takes our minds and thoughts off of a provisional and loving Father, who has provided all we need through Jesus. Fear makes us look at life and ask questions over and over about things we know are concrete in our lives.

Worry will drive us crazy! The answer is to let anxiety drive us to the gospel, where God has dealt with our problems and sins in full. Only in the gospel of Jesus will our out-of-control lives make sense. The gospel takes whatever anxiety distorts and puts our lives back in order. What the enemy stole in the garden is restored by the one who, in his garden of trouble and torment, took our fears, doubts, delusions, and, yes, our worries and dealt with them on a cross. The cross that crushed him frees us, and the tomb that could not hold him gives us resurrection power to face every day, no matter what comes our way. Praise God for such salvation!

Questions for Personal Reflection

1. How has a situation in your life stole your peace?
2. How can focusing on your future in eternity with Christ ease or dispel your fears in this life?
3. What is mean by the phrase, "the joy of abiding in Christ"?

CHAPTER 12
Hidden in the Shadow of the Almighty

The one who lives under the protection of the Most High dwells in the shadow of the Almighty.
—Psalm 91:1

My kids have always loved playing hide-and-seek. Not long ago we had eleven little girls over to our house for my daughter's tenth birthday celebration. Kristina had planned games and crafts and prepared snacks, enough to keep all the princesses busy for four hours. In the middle of all the games, presents, and activities, a giant game of hide-and-seek broke out. Watching a group of fourth-grade girls play hide-and-seek in a three-bedroom house is pretty amazing. We didn't allow them to hide in closets or our bedroom, so they had to get creative. I learned a few things about ten-year-old girls. First, they do things in packs; no one hid alone. They traveled in groups of three or four, so if you found one, then you found a few.

I also found out they are not very good at hide-and-seek. I always thought a good strategy would be to stay silent and still when you are hiding. To me, this increases your odds of not being found. My daughter and her friends, however, liked being found because when someone came within ten feet of their secret spot, they began giggling and snickering. The girls played over and over again, game after game, until finally, they couldn't find a couple of their friends. Our house is not that large, so after a few minutes, their efforts changed from seeking to shouting at their friends to come out.

After a while, I joined in the fun because I didn't want to be the parent who loses track of a few girls in a simple game. After diligently searching, we found the two girls, who declared by their actions that they were incredible at the game. They had opened the door that led to the garage and climbed into my wife's van. We never saw them, and we didn't even think to look for them in the garage.

Like me, you may not be good at "hiding" in the presence of Jesus. Part of winning the battle with your worries resides in where you feel the safest. The safer the place, the quicker you run there. Ask yourself this question: *When fear and anxiety begin to look for me, where do I turn? Where do I go?*

Choose to Live Instead of Visit

Part of allowing the gospel to shape your emotions with regard to worry and anxiety depends on where you choose to take your fears and troubles. One of the tricks the enemy deploys is the trap of isolation. The enemy knows if you are isolated, then the one voice you hear most clearly is his voice and your own. He wants you to be a loner, to figure out by yourself why you are so worried and fearful about life. When you are alone, you tend to be more anxious and worried instead of less anxious and worried.

I think solitude is a very beneficial spiritual exercise. We should get in the habit of taking some time away from the everyday tasks of life to think and ponder life's biggest questions. Spending time in solitude has a way of sharpening the mind and strengthening the inner individual, allowing the Holy Spirit to direct, speak, and act as the wise counsel we need. Let me clarify—solitude and isolation are not two sides of the same coin; they are entirely different currency. You see, isolation focuses on those who isolate themselves, whereas the focus of solitude is a desire to hear from someone else; namely, our heavenly Father.

The person who isolates himself or herself usually is running from a challenge or doesn't want the input and community of others.

The person who finds solitude wants to improve his or her clarity of thought in order to benefit the kingdom of God in a better way.

When we are anxious, we often remove the ability to hear and think clearly. As I've stated, fear and worry will make the situation seem more significant than it is. A lot of times, we can find temporary relief from the plague of anxious living and thinking, and we do this by reading a good book, thinking a positive thought, or listening to encouraging songs. Many believers deal with their anxiety in this way. This reaction is like taking a vacation from life. We take vacations because we need a break from the everyday hustle and bustle. So you go to the beach or the mountains, or maybe you take an adventure or explore a theme park. For a week, you forget about whatever is causing your anxiety. Anxiety may visit you from time to time, but you quickly forget about your troubles because you are on vacation. You now feel like you are out of the reach of anxiety; you have separated yourself, even if for a short time, from those pesky emotions that can weigh down your heart. You feel better—until you come back to reality.

I often have found that when I return to reality, my anxiety is at a higher level than it was before my vacation. I think this is how we deal with things, even on a spiritual level. We vacation in the grace and presence of God, instead of choosing to dwell in the provision, promise, and presence of God. The safety of the existence of God is not something we visit; it's a place we can live. The hope of Psalm 91:1 resides in the peace and rest we find in the presence of God: "To the one who lives under the protection of the Most High."

The Christian experience is not like a getaway for the weekend, an event or experience that helps you forget about your life for a moment. Being a child of God is rooted in the gospel message of the provision made for you in the power of the cross of Christ. His death on the cross allows us to have the protection of the Most High. God himself becomes our refuge, not only for a moment but every day. We have to change the way we view our relationship to God through Jesus, not as something we visit now and then but a well from which we continually draw strength for every challenge. The presence and protection of God provide safety from the anxious thoughts that often challenge us throughout the day.

The Provision of the God Who Dwells

My worry and fear can strike at the most inconvenient times. I'm usually not ready for my feelings of worry, doubt, and fear. They don't ask if they can invade my mind and my soul. A lot of people experience high anxiety when they see change or the threat of change. Professionals attest that high levels of stress and anxious thoughts occur when significant life change happens. Life can be scary; any kind of change is often frightening.

My family has moved a few times over the years, and each time we relocate, it seems our stress level goes up. Yes, we are joyful about the new opportunities and memories we believe are coming our way, but often there is just enough of the unknown to make us experience overwhelming feelings of worry that often lead to dread and despair. I have found that the unknown seems to conjure up more doubt and fear than other situations. The fear of the unknown affects me because I have difficulty trusting. Maybe it's a faith problem, or maybe my expectations are too high, but I struggle with trust.

Because many of us struggle in the same way, we reluctantly choose to be anxious to make a strange and unfamiliar situation more familiar. I have to admit that I am more comfortable with my anxious thoughts than I am with an unclear, different, unknown position. I use my anxiety as more of a security blanket than I would like to admit.

One of the ways we learn to let go of our anxious thoughts is by replacing those habits and behaviors with better ones. Psalm 91:2 states, "I will say concerning the LORD, who is my refuge and my fortress, my God in whom I trust." There is so much truth in this verse. God is more than a security blanket or a coping mechanism. Religion gives us a set of principles and rules to follow, and this can bring security and protection in our lives—but only for a moment. Religion provides a false sense of security, and those who have placed their faith and trust in religion have been disappointed and disillusioned. Christianity is so much more! The Christian faith is not rooted in a system of beliefs or behavior modification techniques. Christianity is about a person, the person of Jesus Christ, who is, who was, and who will always be secure, trustworthy, and someone who will never betray our faith. He is a rescue for the weary and a bulwark against the onslaught of the enemy.

One of the ways we come to understand the provision of God's grace and presence is by understanding how God dwells with his people. There has always been a relational aspect between God and his people. In the garden, God created and had a community with Adam and Eve. Once man fell, and sin entered in, man's relationship was destroyed and cut off. This sin was not just an act but an indwelling, pervasive disease that affected man to the core of his heart.

We are depraved people because of our sinful nature, yet man still found grace in the eyes of the Lord. God made promises to Abraham, Isaac, and Jacob. He prepared a people for himself and sought to deliver them from the bondage they endured in Egypt. In Exodus 3, God revealed himself to Moses, a Hebrew who grew up in Pharaoh's house as YHWH, the great I AM, who desires to dwell with his people. God delivered his people through the leadership of Moses and desired to not only have a relationship with a person but with a community of people. God does not rule from afar. He is near and dwells with his people. God's glory manifests itself in Exodus 40 as a cloud by day and a pillar of fire by night.

> For the cloud of the Lord was over the tabernacle by day, and there was a fire inside the cloud by night, visible to the entire house of Israel throughout all the stages of their journey. (Exodus 40:38)

Did you catch what Exodus 40:38 states about the character of God? Despite the unfaithfulness and nature of the people of God, God never forsook his people, nor did he take his presence from them. He was always faithful, always there. He did not overlook their sins, for there are plenty of times where we see his discipline, but he never took his presence from them. There is always hope embedded in the story of the people of God.

The same is true for us today. Concerning the incarnate Son of God, "The Word became flesh and dwelt among us. We observed his glory, the glory as the one and only Son from the Father, full of grace and truth" (John 1:14). God has chosen to reveal himself to his people through his Word, and there is no greater truth than what is spoken in these verses, as well as in the whole of scripture. We serve a God who dwells with us. He has paid for our sins, our insecurities, our fears, our failures, and, yes, even our anxious ways and thoughts. We find a permanent grace and abiding relationship in Jesus, one who never forsakes or leaves. We can see rest and strength in the shadow of his wing, for the shadow of his sacrifice on the cross covers the length of scripture and the breadth of humanity.

Questions for Personal Reflection

1. What is the difference between hiding in isolation and seeking solitude? Which are you more prone to do?
2. What does it mean to dwell in the provision, promise, and presence of God?
3. How do you respond to the statement that we can be more comfortable with our anxious thoughts than an unclear, different, or unknown position? Do you find this to be true in your life?

CHAPTER 13
Dining in the Presence of the Enemy

You prepare a table before me in the presence of my enemies;
you anoint my head with oil; my cup overflows. Only goodness
and faithful love will pursue me all my days of my life, and
I will dwell in the house of the LORD as long as I live.
—Psalm 23:5–6

My family watched professional wrestling when I was a kid. In the mid-1980s, professional wrestling was very localized. I was born in the South, so a lot of the wrestlers I grew up liking were from places like Atlanta, Georgia, or Charlotte, North Carolina. One of the things I loved about professional wrestling was the way the promoters wrote good storylines. The promoters behind the sport came up with colorful characters and plots that made us enjoy the good guys and dislike the bad guys. Every Saturday night, my family gathered around our television to watch the world of good-versus-evil come to life in a scripted display of athleticism and showmanship. We cheered on our favorites and shook our fists at the bad guys.

One of the things I've noticed about worry is that it makes everything and everyone seem like the bad guy. As I've mentioned, anxiety makes circumstances and situations seem more significant than they are. Worry also can cause conditions, events, and often people look like the enemy. Anxiety and fear often will make us paranoid, making us believe everyone is out to get us. Stress has a way of making everyone and everything the enemy.

Worry and fear affect us all differently. As mentioned, some of us are dealing with crippling anxiety, and the best step for those people is to seek a professional who can help them deal with their struggles. All of us, however, at some point of our journeys, will deal with how worry affects us. Worry can get hold of us by making the things we are facing seem like the enemy. When everyone and everything looks like the enemy, even everyday conversations and situations can cause worry. Have you ever heard someone say, "I wonder what he meant when he said _____ to me"? Or "I don't like the look that person gave me. I wonder if everything is okay between us"? Many of us have spoken with others—or even to ourselves in our heads—about a conversation or encounter that makes us concerned or worried. Often, these thoughts are wrong, or there is some misunderstanding of what has happened. We have allowed a misspoken word to create a distance between us and a good friend, or we have allowed someone's tone to dictate how we act and speak to that person in future conversations.

I have talked to and counseled many who suffer from anxiety that has its root in a misconceived encounter. A lot of times we procrastinate and do not have the crucial conversations we need to have to "clear the air." People may have good relationships, but because of the lack of communication and the anxiety of the moment, good friends can become bitter enemies. I urge you not to allow the worry you feel to dictate the words you say, and don't let the things you do become actions you will later regret. Don't allow the anxiety of the moment to ruin great relationships.

But what about times when we face real enemies? The scriptures are full of people who met real enemies. As God's children, we may face real enemies as well. What do you do when the anxiety you feel about a relationship is real? What about when you meet those who come against you, wanting to see failure or harm come into your life? Let's look at some powerful and comforting truths from Psalm 23 that we can apply to our lives when we face different kinds of enemies.

> I urge you not to allow the worry you feel to dictate the words you say, and don't let the things you do become actions you will later regret.

The Comfort of the Presence of God

Psalm 23 is a very familiar psalm that has provided comfort to the lives of many during times of stress, loss, and grief. The psalm is raw and emotional, teeming with the real-life struggle of the human experience.

> Even when I go through the darkest valley, I fear no danger,
> for you are with me. (Psalm 23:4)

Notice David doesn't say his fear is elevated because his circumstance is pleasant or that all his relationships are healthy. Quite the opposite. David is communicating that even when his times are dark and low, his level of fear is not elevated. Why? The clear meaning of the text leads us to one truth. The presence of God casts this fear aside, allowing David to point us to the comfort of God. The presence of God has a way of bringing happiness to the most challenging places.

Once a wise older pastor gave me a great piece of advice regarding the comfort that God's presence can bring. He told me that my presence as a pastor could bring some level of satisfaction, but I should not make the mistake of thinking it could bring ultimate peace and comfort to a situation. I could help and I could support, and I might bring hope and peace with my words and actions, but they will be short-lived. On the other hand, the gospel of Christ offers a person an eternal solution. The greatest comfort one can find is in the Prince of Peace, Jesus Christ, who has walked through the darkest valley of the cross and gives us the life-giving grace of the resurrection.

The Comfort of the Provision of God

One of the mistakes I make in my relationship with God is that I think God's provision is not big enough for whatever I'm experiencing. I believe Jesus is just holding me as I go through the rough moments of my life. Sometimes when I am going through a difficult time, I picture Jesus covering me up until the storm passes over. When my children are scared, I do the same thing; I protect them in the best way I can from the things they see as dangerous. I can remember holding them when a strong storm rolled through the area, or I picked them up when they were in an uncomfortable and scary situation. As admirable and comforting as these actions are, they fail in comparison to the provision God provides.

God's rule does not start when the storm ends; we can experience his control in the depths of our troubles. Don't underestimate the power of this truth. You can experience the depth of God's love and grace in the presence of your enemies, and then you can experience it by his taking you out of the existence of your enemies. We may pray for the Lord to deliver us from our enemies, to take their power and control away from us. This reaction is normal. No one wants to suffer at the hands of someone who intends harm.

Psalm 23:5 states, "You prepare a table before me in the presence of my enemies." A table is a place of community and provision. A table welcomes weary souls to dine and refresh themselves with food and drink from a kind and friendly host. A table is a place of conversation and laughter. A table is what God sets before his children in the presence of their enemies. God delights in making provision and in giving himself to his children in the darkest times. When we realize there is a table of grace in the midst of our enemies, our minds and thoughts can run to the one who sets the table, instead of those who surround the table.

> When we realize there is a table of grace in the midst of our enemies, our minds and thoughts can run to the one who sets the table, instead of those who surround the table.

The truth found here has brought great comfort to my soul when it could easily have become distracted by the outside influences, whose desire is to harm and not to heal.

The Comfort of the Pursuit of God

David is the writer of Psalm 23. First and Second Samuel record much of David's life, and we see a man who spent a lot of time running from his enemies. King Saul desired to destroy David.

> Every day Jesse's son lives on earth you and your kingship are not secure. Now send for him and bring him to me-he must die! (1 Samuel 20:31)

King Saul was not David's only threat. As a youth, David faced bears, lions, and even a giant warrior named Goliath, who said, "I'll give your flesh to the birds of the sky and the wild beasts!" (1 Samuel 17:44). We see the deliverance and provision of the Lord throughout David's life, even when his circumstances were dire. David proclaimed it wasn't his enemies who pursued him during most of his life; he said that only God's "goodness and faithful love" pursued him. We might think he would have recounted all of his enemies and the trials he faced, but instead, he spoke of the unfailing love of the God of Israel as his pursuer. I think this is how grace works; it lifts our eyes from the everyday trials that make us scared, worried, and anxious and helps us recount how many times these trials were not faced alone. Anxiety cannot keep up with the grace of God.

The grace of God will always outrun and outlast the things we worry about the most. Hold on, and embrace this great truth. We can either turn our eyes to the hard stuff in our lives, or we can see the abundant love of Christ in hot pursuit of his children.

> Anxiety cannot keep up with the grace of God.

Questions for Personal Reflection

1. How does it feel when you believe your enemies are stronger than your God?
2. How has the presence of God comforted you when you have experienced anxiety?
3. How has the grace of God relieved your anxiety?

CHAPTER 14
A Better Way

Therefore I tell you; Don't worry about your life, what you will eat or what you will drink; or about your body, what you will wear. Isn't life more than food and the body more than clothing?
—Matthew 6:25

Remember that anxiety cannot keep up with the grace of God, but anxiety seems to outpace us every day. As we live, we can easily fall prey to the worries of the day. We spend our time worrying about what is around the next corner. We worry about what our kids will face over the next twenty-four hours. We read an email, and we worry about the assumed tone the sender is conveying. We worry about which bills the postman will deliver or the thought of someone hacking our identity and plunging us into financial ruin. Are you worried yet? You see, there are plenty of things to worry about, and we could spend countless hours fearing the known and the unknown. The number of the things that make us anxious is exhausting and never-ending. Have you ever wondered if there is a better way to live life, one without worrying? Jesus gives us that better way in Matthew 6:5–34.

The Sermon on the Mount resounds with words of challenge and comfort. Jesus, like the prophet Moses before him, speaks from a mountain, delivering the words of God, but unlike Moses, who was a man sent by God, this man is God himself. His words are clear but challenging, making us think, *Who can live this way?* A quick read through Matthew 5–7 leads to only one conclusion: we can't do this on our own. Jesus doesn't lower the bar. He raises the bar outside of the reach of religion, morality, and proper behavior. Jesus makes it clear that those who will inherit the kingdom of God must be poor in spirit. The people of the kingdom of God have one thing in common: they all need Jesus. And it's the same for you and me when it comes to our anxieties. We all need Jesus to deal with them.

Don't Worry about the Needs of Today

Jesus cut straight to the point in Matthew 6:25 when he said, "Don't worry about your life." A lot of the things we worry about have to do with us. We may worry about others, but if we are honest, worry tends to show up at the threshold of our own houses. Daily anxiety tends to camp out around the daily activities of life. I have noticed this in my own life and the lives of others. We worry just as much over the smaller, everyday details as over the more significant, life-changing moments in our lives. Jesus instructs us not to worry about three daily needs: what we will drink, what we will eat, and what we will wear. Plenty of people need these three, and plenty of people have an abundance of them. Which are you?

Check your closets. How much clothing does your family own? Is it enough to get through the day? We may not worry about the amount of clothing we own as much as the type of clothing. There is a thin line between our needs and our desires, and once our desires get out of control, our emotions will soon follow, creating anxious thoughts, which can lead to a worrisome lifestyle.

Open your fridge. How much food and drink do you have? There are people who do not have adequate food, but most of the worry comes from hearts that are centered on ourselves. Where is our food? Where is our drink? Where are our provisions?

I have to confess that I worry the most about myself. I am consumed with my life, my stipulations, my heartache, my circumstances, and my feelings. A lot of this anxiety comes from the idea that if no one will take care of me, then I have to take care of myself. This individualistic way of thinking and living can quickly hinder a believer's life. We begin to think wrong thoughts concerning the way God views us. God, who is rich in love and has provided everything we need from him in Jesus, reminds us of an important truth that can extinguish our anxiety:

> Consider the birds of the sky: They don't sow or reap or gather into barns, yet your heavenly Father feeds them. Aren't you worth more than they? (Matthew 6:26)

Jesus points his hearers to the loving Father who, since creation, has provided for his creation. He looks to the birds of the air and asks his audience to take note of the provision God has made for them; then he asks a searing question: Aren't you worth more than they?

Anxiety can often measure how much you believe you are worth to God.

A lot of our worry stems from how little our identities rest in the finished work of Jesus Christ. Our identities are often wrapped up in what we have; this is why we worry about our provisions. A person's worth is not found in his or her present circumstances, income, provisions, or status. A person's worth is found in how much God loves and cares for him or her. One of the fundamental truths we forget is that God loves us.

> Anxiety can often measure how much you believe you are worth to God.

I have walked with people through really tragic circumstances. Some of them were going through a divorce or the death of a loved one. Some had been fired from a job that had given them security for decades, and now they were facing an entirely new life. Trying circumstances can block our ability to know, understand, and believe that God loves us. Anxiety then becomes an operating system for navigating life, so instead of living life through the lens of the gospel, we view life through the lens of what is happening to us at the moment; this can lead to anxiety. We need perspective—and a perspective grander and wiser than our own.

The words of Jesus are good, and we need to hear them. The devil attempts to convince God's children that God does not love them, and therefore God will not provide for them. One of the devil's tactics is to point at what you are experiencing daily as proof that the love of God is a farce or a fairy tale for misguided, insecure, bewildered humans. We have to believe the Word of God more than the lies of the enemy.

The scriptures do not promise a comfortable life for the followers of Jesus. The apostle Paul explains this concept:

> Therefore we do not give up. Even though our outer person is being destroyed, our inner person being is renewed day by day. For our momentary light affliction is producing for us an absolutely incomparable eternal weight of glory. (2 Corinthians 4:16–17)

What encouragement we receive from this promise. Anxiety shouts, "Worry about your life! Worry about your future!" Anxiety wants us to fear what will happen to us—the outer person. God's Word says the opposite. God's Word reminds us that God will use even the things that produce anxiety to form and renew our inner persons on a day-to-day basis. God's provision, love, and message renew the believer every day. The gospel of Jesus gives us hope for tomorrow, changes our perspective for today, and enables us to believe in a brighter future.

Paul states that many of us are suffering from "momentary light afflictions," or MLAs. We all have MLAs in our lives. They creep in and steal the joy and love of life so easily, but we have to acknowledge the truth about MLAs—we may be suffering from afflictions, but they are momentary and light, even if they don't feel like they are. I don't want to minimize what anyone goes through, but we can all take comfort in this truth in the scriptures.

Remember that our emotions can quickly get out of control, but the gospel can rein them in. When we look at the cross, we see a man who took the weight of real affliction for his children. Jesus paid for the sin of humanity on the cross, and our MLAs do not compare with the pain and suffering he endured. Jesus took the weight of our sins so that we could experience, as Paul states, "an incomparable eternal weight of glory."

When we see what is happening to our outer person, we often become anxious, but when we look at the inner person, who is strengthened each day by the Holy Spirit through the provision of Jesus, our anxieties can fade away.

God Knows What You Need

In the latter part of Matthew 6, the gospel shapes how we might react to the MLAs we experience each day.

> For the Gentiles eagerly seek all these things, and your heavenly Father knows that you need them. But seek first the kingdom of God and his righteousness and all these things will be provided for you. (Matthew 6:32–33)

We have to remind ourselves always that God knows what he is doing, and he knows what we need. Anxiety often tells us to run after the things of the world. Worry will make us believe that we will never have enough, so the answer is to get more stuff. The problem with this is that we will never find the security we need by chasing after all the things we think we need. Think of buying a new pair of shoes and then worrying about getting them dirty. When I was a teenager, I got a new pair of shoes but kept them in the box because I knew they would get scuff marks on them as soon as I wore them.

Worry can cause you to fear life so much that you don't even embrace the life God has for you every day. What is the answer? It's simple: acknowledge that your heavenly Father knows what you need. He knows what you will experience, and he knows all the things you need to get you through the day. Don't worry about tomorrow; rest in his presence today. Don't worry if you will have enough. Your Father will provide what you need, although maybe not what you want. Look to him for your provisions, for he is trustworthy and kind. Don't worry about tomorrow. It has enough trouble of its own. Look to God's provision for today.

Questions for Personal Reflection

1. What is your biggest worry?
2. How has this worry affected your daily life?
3. How can you recover from MLAs?

CHAPTER 15
The Antidote for an Anxious Life

Don't worry about anything, but in everything, through prayer and petition with thanksgiving, present your requests to God. And the peace of God, which surpasses all understanding, will guard your hearts and minds in Christ Jesus.
—Philippians 4:6–7

So it's simple—don't worry about your life. God's has a plan, and he will accomplish his plan, with or without us. But what happens when we forget about his promises, his truth, and his love for us? How do we embrace the hope we have in Jesus, the reality of the gospel, while remembering we have an eternal Father who will never leave or forsake his children? Often anxiety has a boomerang effect on a person. That is, anxiety will seemingly retreat, only to come back to attack our emotions with reinforcements. Anxiety and worry constantly will attack until they take hold of our entire persons, forcing their will upon our minds and hearts. Anxiety wants to make us prisoners, locking us away in a dark dungeon, away from the light of the presence of God, and forcing us to worry whether anyone knows or understands our situations.

Remember that worry and fear have a way of making the unknown seem scarier and more significant than it is.

Anxiety wants to hide the light of God's presence from our lives so our faith is weak, and our emotions are out of control. Worry grows best in the soil of a forgetful heart—a heart where the pages of God's faithfulness are forgotten and replaced

> Remember that worry and fear have a way of making the unknown seem scarier and more significant than it is.

by the breaking news of a turbulent and unpredictable future. When we forget God's promises, we envision situations with frightful outcomes, and this is a recipe for disaster. This way of thinking generally happens in a few different ways. God has promised, "I will never leave you or abandon you" (Hebrews 13:5), but our emotions tell us, *God is not there; He doesn't know what you are going through.*

God promises in Isaiah 54:10, "Though the mountains move and the hills shake, my love will not be removed from you, and my covenant of peace will not be shaken, says your compassionate LORD," but our emotions tell us, *God doesn't love you. He doesn't understand, and it's up to you to figure out this life on your own.*

God promises that he will forgive our sin if we acknowledge and confess our sin.

> If we confess our sins, he is faithful and righteous to forgive us our sins and to cleanse us from all unrighteousness. (1 John 1:9)

But our emotions speak to our hearts and say, *Your sin is too much, too heinous, too egregious to forgive.* Again and again, these scenarios play over in our minds and hearts, leaving us with a question: will we believe what God has to say about us, or will we believe what worry and fear have to say? Paul dealt with the same struggle in the early church, and his writings to the church in Philippi have good instructions for the fickle hearts we deal with today.

Chose Prayer Over Worry

Christianity is not the only belief system that sees the importance of prayer, but Christianity is the single belief system that paints the picture of a God who is near. In Philippians 4:5, Paul reminds his fellow believers of the nearness of God. Theologians use two words to help people wrap their minds around God's location: *transcendence* and *immanence*.

We use the word *transcendence* to describe how God is not like us. He is above all things, and we are separated from his glory and his presence. Isaiah 55:8–9 speaks of God's transcendence:

> For my thoughts are not your thoughts, and your ways are not my ways. This is the Lord's declaration. For as heaven is higher than earth, so my ways are higher than your ways, and my thoughts than your thoughts.

These words accentuate what theologians have written for centuries; namely, God is not like us in so many ways. God's way of thinking and living is far above our ways. God's transcendence explains why God feels so distant from our everyday lives, which, in a sense, he is. God operates on an entirely different level from humanity, and while this truth brings his children comfort, it also can make his presence seem distant and foggy.

Theologians also use *immanence* to describe the Lord. God's immanence means he is close to his children, and this does not merely indicate location. God is beyond location, space, and time. God operates outside these natural boundaries. We can rest in the fact that while God is transcendent and reigns over his entire creation, he is also immanent and close to his people.

> From one man he has made every nationality to live over the whole earth and has determined their appointed times and the boundaries where they live. He did this so that they might seek God, and perhaps they may reach out and find him though he is not far from each one of us. (Acts 17:26–27)

The nearness of God is a powerful truth for us to consider. Because he is close, we can reach out to him in prayer. Our prayers go beyond the limitations of our words and our circumstances. Sometimes we may feel that our prayers don't get off the ground, that they can't reach his ear, but that is not the reality of those who find themselves in Christ. Because God is immanent, he can hear our prayers and respond perfectly. Our worry finds no place to grow because of the closeness of God and his ability to understand and answer our prayers.

Paul urges the church to pray because of that truth. He can say with confidence that we should not worry about anything but pray about everything, yet here is where the difficulty comes. *Many of God's people choose not to believe God's Word.* They worry about everything and pray about nothing. A poor prayer life will always lead to an overburdened, worry-filled life. We shouldn't just pray about everything; we should pray about everything with thanksgiving. Presenting everything to God with prayer and thanksgiving will keep a check on our anxiety levels. When we worry about our kids, we must take the time to pray for them. When we worry about our future, we must take the time to pray about it. What would it look like if every decision, situation, and worry was bathed in prayer before the Father? Our emotions would radically change if prayer were our first response instead of our last option.

> Many of God's people choose not to believe God's Word. They worry about everything and pray about nothing.

The Lasting Benefit of Prayer

Why does it benefit a person to pray? Does prayer change things? Many of us look at prayer as plan B instead of plan A. We use prayer as a final option when all other options have been exhausted, yet the scriptures see prayer as the first option when faced with choices, difficulties, and decisions. Nehemiah prays for success before he asks the king for permission to repair the walls of Jerusalem. Solomon prays and asks for wisdom before he begins his reign as king of Israel. Paul prays for an open door before he sets off on one of his several missionary journeys. The church has a rich history of God's people calling out to God before they are faced with obstacles.

We seek before we act because prayer should precede our endeavors, instead of being the last resort when our attempts are failing. Our everyday worries would lessen if we understood the power of prayer. Regarding the benefits of prayer, Paul writes, "And the peace of God, which surpasses all understanding, will guard your hearts and minds in Christ Jesus" (Philippians 4:7). Paul is writing from a Roman prison, so he not only understands the power of these words on a divine plane but a practical and personal one as well.

God uses prayer to secure peace in our minds and hearts, even when our lives look like a war zone.

> God uses prayer to secure peace in our minds and hearts, even when our lives look like a war zone.

The people of God would wish peace, or "shalom," to those they dearly loved. Peace was a hope and prayer for all things to go well with an individual. This peace is what our relationship with Christ brings to each believer. The death of Christ brings more shalom to an individual than all the prophets, priests, and kings in the history of Israel tried to obtain. This peace is not only protection and security from the trials of life, but it also can settle our hearts and minds while we go through the trials of life. The peace of God could reach Paul in a prison cell, and it can reach you in the calamity you are facing today. God's peace also surpasses our abilities to reason why we feel so peaceful in certain situations. The peace God brings to his children trumps what we think about our circumstances. How does God's peace prevail in our lives? Paul gives the reason in Philippians 4:7—our hearts can remain at rest because they are guarded in Christ Jesus.

When I was single, many well-meaning believers told me to guard my heart when it came to interacting with potential romantic relationships. This advice came from Proverbs 4:23, which says, "Guard your heart above all else, for it is the source of life." This verse may leave us with a question: how do we guard our hearts? Practically, we can lock our hearts away and never allow anyone to hurt us by denying them access to our hearts. Author and lay theologian C. S. Lewis gave wise words concerning this plan:

> Love anything, and your heart will certainly be wrung and possibly broken. If you want to make sure of keeping it intact, you must give your heart to no one, not even to an animal. Wrap it carefully round with hobbies and little luxuries; avoid all entanglements; lock it up safe in the casket or coffin of your selfishness. But in that casket-safe, dark, motionless, airless-it will change. It will not be broken; it will become unbreakable, impenetrable, irredeemable.[3]

Did you catch what Lewis said about locking your heart way? It becomes unbreakable and, sadly, irredeemable. I'm not advocating giving your heart away to just anyone. Israel gave their hearts to idols, and this practice destroyed the nation and the people. We need to protect our hearts because the heart is the wellspring of life. Christianity has a solution to this problem, and his name is Jesus. Jesus not only redeems our hearts, but he also guards our hearts and our minds. When we are "in" Christ, our minds and our hearts have a safe place to love and grow. We do not have to be our own protection when we have the King of kings protecting our emotions. Anxiety and worry will try to creep in, but we can realize that the promises and protection Jesus offers is a much better way of looking at life than our worry and anxiety affords.

I tend to worry much more than I should. Perhaps you would say the same. I know who I am in Christ, and my identity rests securely in him, yet the little worries of the day tend to choke out the good words from God that I need so desperately. So what should we do? We should fix our eyes on Jesus, and through regular, consistent, intentional prayer, we take every matter, every worry, and every sin, and we deposit them at his loving feet. He never tires of his children coming to his throne.

Questions for Personal Reflection

1. How does prayer aid in your worry?
2. What are some of the lasting benefits of prayer that you have experienced? Write down these benefits.
3. How do you practically guard your heart?

CHAPTER 16
Where Does Joy Originate?

My whole source of joy is in you.
—Psalm 87:7

Up to this point, the focus has been on emotions with a more negative tendency. We want to limit anger and anxiety in most situations. We want protective barriers and walls because anxious and angry people can harm themselves and others. But what about joy? Do we want to limit joy? Can we have too much joy in our lives?

As I write, the valley in which I live is coated with a foot of snow. I have noticed that snow and winter weather brings out either the worst or the best in people. For example, some people become anxious during winter weather. They worry about their supplies of food, the conditions of the roads, and staying warm during the night. They wake up plagued by questions like, "What will I do if the heat pump goes out? What if I run out of bread and milk? What if my kids can't get to school?"

Then there are the angry winter-weather people. These people despise the winter weather. They can't wait until spring, when they don't have to put up with the winter season. Their social-media feed is filled with a countdown to spring and beach-inspired memes. They don't like the snow, the salt on the roads, or the brisk, cold air.

Then there are my kids. When they see the snowfall, their hearts jump for joy. Nothing can erase the smiles on their faces as they bundle up, grab their sleds, and run outside to enjoy the freshly fallen snow. Should I limit their joy? Does their father tell them not to enjoy the snow too much? No, I want them to find joy in so many experiences, like holidays, snowy days, visits from grandparents, freshly made cookies, playing with friends, and a host of other experiences where they find joy.

The problem with joy is that, like other emotions, it attaches itself to someone or something else. Joy is often spawned by a person, a place, or an experience, and unlike anger and anxiety, it is the absence of the person, place, or experience that makes our joy cease. Usually, if we are removed from whatever or whoever is making us angry or anxious, then those emotions subside, but remove us from the person, place, or experience in which we find joy, and often our joy turns into anger, fear, and worry.

For instance, take children away from whatever makes them anxious and afraid, like a dark room, or a scary sound and the anxiety and fear will leave. It may take some time, but their emotions will calm down. Take something away from them that causes joy, like their favorite toy and their happiness quickly goes, and other emotions—like fear, anger, or anxiety—ramp up. The reason our joy quickly subsides is not that our joy was wrong but that it was misplaced.

We misplace joy when we root joy in only temporary things. Most things that give joy have expiration dates, causing joy to last only a short while, especially when compared to eternity. Although we can find joy in people, places, and experiences, our joy should be tempered by the pleasure that comes from something outside the natural boundaries of time and space. We can find happiness in a lot of places, but let's look at two broad categories where we find joy: people and places.

> We misplace joy when we root joy in only temporary things.

The Joy We Find in People

I enjoy the relationships and friends I have made over the years. My wife asked me to help her with a list of people to whom we should send Christmas cards, and the process was quite tedious. First, I had to make a list, then I had to find the addresses, and then I had to go back over the list to see if I had forgotten anyone. We have served five churches over the past twenty-three years of ministry. Searching for addresses and making this list allowed me to take a trip down memory lane as I thought about all the good, Christlike people I have come to know as friends. I recalled so many times of joy and happiness, as God brought each special relationship I had over the years.

Paul writes to the church in Philippi, "I give thanks to my God for every remembrance of you, always praying with joy for all of you" (Philippians 1:3–4). You see, it is good to find joy in relationships. Church families are so blessed to have one another. We comfort one another, help one another, pray for one another, and encourage one another in the faith. Relationships are complex and not always easy. Disagreements in the church can abound, and selfishness may prevail, but I have found so much joy in the people of God over the years.

It's not only the people of God who bring joy into our lives. Easily, I find the most joy in the relationships I have through the family God has given me. For some people, the word *family* does not make them joyful. Sin can enter into any relationship and twist and mangle something God meant for good, causing harm and bitterness. Not all families are good. Because of sin, we often shipwreck the precious relationships God desired to use in our lives to shape us into the image of his Son.

I, however, have experienced some of the greatest moments of joy with my little family. In 2 Samuel 7:18, David speaks of the Lord's faithfulness to his family: "Then King David went in, sat in the LORD's presence, and said, Who am I, Lord God, and what is my house that you have brought me this far?" I experience some of the same emotions when I think about the family God has given me. The greatest joy I have on this earth is experienced with my wife and kids. I have enjoyed every nighttime song, every dinner, every school sporting event, and every conversation and adventure. The days are sometimes long, but the years are short—and there is the problem. Preschool years are replaced by elementary schoolyears and then middle and high school years. Then kids move out and maybe even away, and nothing is the same.

Even family is short-lived. Throughout my forty-plus years, I have enjoyed relationships, and I have seen some connections come to an end. Every relationship we have on this earth is temporary, at best. God has fixed the times and places for people to live.

> Since a person's days are determined and the number of his months depends on you, and since you have set limits he cannot pass. (Job 14:5)

All relationships are temporary. I have seen death take a sister and a mother during my lifetime. It doesn't mean I don't have memories filled with joy; it just means those moments of pleasure were temporary. Separation, divorce, death, and sin can destroy relationships and—if we are not careful—the joy we have in these relationships. We all should pray for and pursue good, God-honoring relationships in our lives, but if we place all of our happiness in relationships, then we will be disappointed at some time.

The Joy We Find in Places

I love waking in the morning and having a cup of coffee at my kitchen table. I wake early, when the house is tranquil, and I can enjoy the first moments of the day in peace. I look forward to the place at my table. Most of us have a place we like to go. It may be the beach, the mountains, or our favorite restaurant or coffee shop. Just like the relationships we have, these places can bring us joy. My family is spread out over four states, so we can't all drop by for family dinners. Occasionally, my wife's family will all meet at the beach to enjoy time together, so the beach is one of our favorite places to go.

God valued specific locations, especially in the Old Testament. In Genesis 12:1, God speaks these words to Abraham: "The Lord said to Abram: Go out from your land, your relatives, and your father's house to the land that I will show you." Here, we see God moving Abraham (Abram) from one place to another place. Also, we see the people of Israel yearning for land or a place to call their own. God gives the people this place in the land of Canaan and reminds them it is he, by his grace, who has provided a place for them.

In Deuteronomy 6:10, God reminds the nation, "When the Lord your God brings you into the land he swore to your fathers, Abraham, Isaac, and Jacob that he would give you- a land with large and beautiful cities that you did not build."

Again, God delivered a land to the nation, one filled with all that the people of God would need for a joyful existence, yet this was temporary. We find, generations later, that idols had captured the hearts of the people, and God took the land away from his people. They are carried off into captivity, away from the joy of the land.

In Psalm 137, we see the people of Babylon asking to hear the songs sung when the people of Israel occupied the land, and we also see the response to this request: "How can we sing the Lord's song on foreign soil? If I forget you Jerusalem, may my right hand forget its skill" (Psalm 137:4–5).

Throughout scripture, we see the importance the people of God put on places and dwellings. There is nothing wrong with enjoying a particular area. Home should be a place that brings joy. We should find joy in gathering together in a place to worship the Lord each week. Our hometowns should bring us joy. It's great to visit and see different locations, yet some of us place too much emphasis on locations. We may allow our joy to be rooted in a place. Again, the problem is that these locations are temporary. Vacations last a certain amount of time, or we may have to move away from the perfect location in the ideal city. We may never get to go back to that one place that made our hearts soar. Places, just like relationships, have an expiration date, unless they are rooted in the eternal. Remember God's words to Abraham—to go to a place he would show him. The writer of Hebrews gives us insight into the cause of Abraham's obedience and the call of God.

> By faith he stayed as a foreigner in the land of promise, living in tents as did Isaac and Jacob, coheirs of the same promise. For he was looking forward to the city that has foundations, whose architect and builder is God. (Hebrews 11:9–10)

Our joy is short-lived because even the best locations and places on this earth are like "living in tents." These places are not our final destinations, and when we convince ourselves that there is nothing more than these places where we can go in this temporary life, then we misplace our joy and put it somewhere it never was supposed to be. Every place we go on this earth is limited by time, but not the eternal home. The city that was designed by God will give us an eternal joy that the best place on earth could never give.

People and places are not the only things that make us joyful and happy. There are a host of other experiences where we find joy. Yet the ultimate joy is not found in family, homes, travel, or the right relationship. The only true lasting joy comes from the giver of all good things, the eternal God. Psalm 87:7 testifies to this truth. A person's entire joy comes from knowing and seeking God.

Our joy can easily attach itself to temporary pleasures, but these are fleeting at best and can't deliver like the God of the universe. True joy comes only from him.

Questions for Personal Reflection

1. What makes you happy?
2. What is the difference between joy and happiness?
3. What brings you more joy: people or places? Why?

CHAPTER 17
When Joy Withers

Though the fig tree does not bud and there is no fruit on the vines, though the olive crop fails and the fields produce no food, though the flocks disappear from the pen and there are no herds in the stalls, yet I will celebrate in the Lord; I will rejoice in the God of my salvation!
—Habakkuk 3:17–18

I once received a text from a friend that read, "Can you meet with friends of mine? They need help." A couple, long-time friends of my friend, were walking through a difficult time in their marriage. During the meeting, we talked through the situation they were facing. When I asked what they believed was wrong, one of them said, "I'm not happy anymore."

Many of us have been there, whether it's marriage, our jobs, raising kids, or any other endeavor, we all have to face the question: "How do I go on when I'm not happy in my situation?" There will be times in our Christian journey when life is not fun, pleasant, or enjoyable. What do we do during these times? The writings of the prophet Habakkuk offer encouragement as we face times when our joy is withering.

Habakkuk wrote during the fall and decline of the Judean kingdom. Jerusalem was surrounded by the army of Babylon and would finally fall in 612 BC. Israel's economy and influence gathered momentum under King Josiah, who died in 609 BC, and then the nation was faced with deportation and a loss of property, national pride, and heritage.

The book of Habakkuk traces God's judgment during this time, while offering a glimpse of the future grace the Lord provides as he holds the declining rebelling nation in his right hand. The prophet's writing in

Habakkuk 3 offers answers to two questions: How do I find joy when my security is taken away, and how do I celebrate in the midst of trials?

When Our Joy Is Attached to Our Security

Everyone wants to feel safe *and* be safe. We take our security very seriously today. We purchase software to protect our identity on the internet. We buy insurance to provide for us in case we lose our homes or have an accident while traveling. We enlist the services of security companies that monitor our properties on a twenty-four-hour basis. We install cameras on our front doors and can check on the safety of our property from another location.

One might make the case that safety and security are more important to society than at any other time in history. Perhaps it's the violence we see daily through the news or social media. The threat of losing life, property, or security is real, so we take every precaution to ensure nothing wrong will happen. But what if the unthinkable happens? Does our joy and faith wither when uncertainty and chaos ensues?

We all must face an unsettling truth: we can't ensure our security and protection. No insurance company can protect us from harm and calamity. No government can promise perfect safety and security in this current world. The most expensive monitoring system or antivirus software cannot keep our investments and property perfectly safe. I'm not advocating a cavalier attitude when it comes to safety and security. We should take every precaution to ensure the safety and protection of those we love and care for, yet we face an often frightening reality—natural disasters happen; the economy can fail; a phone call can change our lives in an instant. When we base our security on the ability to keep order by ourselves, our security will someday fail. None of us wants to lose what we treasure. Jesus understood this principle. We love what we cherish.

Jesus said:

> Don't store up for yourselves treasures on earth, where moth and rust destroy and where thieves break in and steal. But store up for yourselves treasures in heaven, where neither moth nor rust destroys and where thieves don't break in and steal. (Matthew 6:19–20)

Jesus has reminded us of a simple truth; our treasures on this earth can be stolen and destroyed, and our joy will meet the same fate if it is attached only to this temporary existence.

Why? Because we can't ensure the security of the things we hold precious here on earth. Habakkuk's writings remind us of the same principle from another perspective. Sometimes the things we treasure are not taken from us all at once; they may wither in front of our eyes. Marriages can sometimes self-destruct in an instant after an unwise and sinful action, but they can also deteriorate over an extended period. We can ruin relationships in an instant with an outburst of anger, or we can neglect them and watch them die over the years. When we lose something in an instant, the shock of the situation is powerful, but expected. When we lose something in segments, we often are surprised but equally devastated; this was what the people experienced in Habakkuk's day.

Withering Joy

Israel's economy thrived because the land produced for the needs of the country. The vine, the tree, and the herd were all vital to the success of the country. The land the people occupied was given to them by the grace of God, and the success and productivity they needed to sustain them came from the land's ability to produce. Drought, famine, and enemy conquest were all real threats to the economic engine of Israel. Author Robert L. Alden gives helpful insight into the situation described in Habakkuk 3:17. He says, "The nouns used in this verse represent the bases of Israel's agricultural economy. Here prosperity was dependent on the nation's obedience to the covenant and on the Lord's consequent blessing."[4] The prosperity of the nation depended on two things: their obedience and the faithfulness of the Lord.

We likely will find our joy shipwrecked when we drift into the sea of disobedience. Disobedience doesn't always show itself in tangible ways, but it's relatively easy to recognize unethical behavior. The Bible gives clear warnings regarding the outward expression of rebellion to God's law, such as lies, slander, unfaithfulness, covetousness, and sexual immorality. We can't expect the blessings of God when we do not fear the holiness of God. If we are not careful, we can descend into the mire of legalism, expecting that we are justified before God's throne by our sheer adherence to the law of God, his ethical and moral code, and our ability to keep the two. Legalism will not lead to the blessing of God, nor will it provide the joy he desires in our lives. Legalism will slowly drain the life from a person.

Many expect that being a good Christian and doing all the right things should be enough to establish joy in their lives. Sadly, this is only part of the equation—yes, only part. God would not have given his commandments to his people if he didn't expect them to follow obediently. Jesus said, "If you love me, you will keep my commands" (John 14:15). Jesus makes it clear that part of our relating to him in an abiding relationship is in our keeping his commandments, yet many have denied this with their lifestyles, in response to the fear of legalism.

Legalism does not mean we have a strict conformity to God's rules; legalism means we forfeit the grace of God, shown through the cross, with our feeble attempts to please God on our own. Because God's people were rebelling against him, the land rebelled against the people over several generations. Israel saw great promise, but the promise crumbled as they saw the land wither away. We may lose our joy over a time that corresponds with how seriously we take our obedience to God. John Rosemond, a popular family psychologist, sees this same principle at work in the lives of children. He writes, "The most obedient children are also the happiest children."[5] The same goes for us, the children of God. We have more joy in our lives when we are obedient than when we are disobedient.

The success of Israel didn't depend solely on their obedience but also on the faithfulness of God to his covenant. We can see the gospel with much clarity here. One of the themes of the book of Habakkuk is waiting patiently on the Lord. Habakkuk is praying to the Lord in chapter 1, and the prophet begins chapter 2

> Legalism does not mean we have a strict conformity to God's rules; legalism means we forfeit the grace of God, shown through the cross, with our feeble attempts to please God on our own.

with these words: "I will stand at my guard post and station myself on the lookout tower. I will watch to see what he will say to me."

The prophet is in a posture of waiting before the Lord. Some of us are in this posture, waiting for something—some word, some situation—to change, and then we will be happy again. Realize, though, that your joy may *not* change just because your situation changes; moreover, you are not guaranteed a change in your circumstance.

We often hold our joy for ransom, waiting on God to change something we need changing. Our role is to be obedient and faithful; God will change things when he desires to change things. The sooner we, as his children, learn this principle, the sooner we will experience greater joy in this life. Why? Because joy is not predicated on circumstances; joy is dependent on the object to which joy is attached, and the best place to attach our joy is in the provision of God; namely, in Jesus Christ. The prophet gives us insight into where joy can find a place to be nourished and won't dry up.

> Yet I will celebrate in the LORD; I will rejoice in the God
> of my salvation! (Habakkuk 3:18)

Christianity is the only religion for which its followers rejoice in the face of adversity—not because of their faithfulness but because of the faithfulness of the God of their salvation. Salvation will not come when the vine, tree, or herd is fruitful again. Salvation comes from the root of David, King Jesus, the one Isaiah wrote about in Isaiah 11:1, "Then a shoot will grow from the stump of Jesse, and a branch from his roots will bear fruit."

God is so faithful and powerful that he alone can provide the security and salvation we need. He provided a branch that bears fruit from a stump—one who comes as the Lamb of God who takes away the sin of the world. This branch is Jesus, and we have been grafted into his story by the gospel. Paul wrote, "You, through a wild olive branch, were grafted in among them and have come to share in the rich root of the cultivated olive tree" (Romans 11:17). Paul gives us a beautiful picture of the grace of God, grafting us into the branch that is Jesus, and now we bear fruit to his glorious name.

So it doesn't matter if your joy is withering today. His faithfulness will endure and never wither. His promise is sure; his provision is enough. Joy is found in Jesus, our faithful King!

Questions for Personal Reflection

1. What does it feel like to lose your joy?
2. What makes your joy wither?
3. Do you struggle with legalism? Explain.

CHAPTER 18
When You Fight for Your Joy and the Joy of Others

*But we are workers with you for your joy,
because you stand firm in your faith.
—2 Corinthians 1:24*

We don't wake up every day in a good mood. We may find ourselves facing a day we do not want to meet and conversations we do not want to have. A lot of us dread what may be around the corner. We may dread the attitude our kids give us upon waking. We may fear a project deadline . Maybe we are too exhausted to meet the day. Each day brings its triumphs and its tragedies. How do we fight to remain joyful, despite the events and challenges of the day? How do we stand firm in the convictions we have developed as believers, work out our faith, and endure all things with joy? We fight for what we believe in. We fight for what we think is true, beautiful, and right, and we fight for what love. Jesus tells his followers in Matthew 6:34, "Each day has enough trouble of its own." We do not know what each day will bring; all we can hope for is an idea, so we plan and make provisions for what may come.

One thing we can count on is that we will have to fight for joy because some of the things we will face will be less than favorable. The apostle Paul realized seeking joy didn't come naturally, and he gave the church in Corinth some things to think about as they fought for their joy.

First, Preach the Gospel to Yourself

As stated earlier, we may have to fight sometimes for the joy we have in Christ. This fight is active, not passive. We can't expect to be joyful if we don't engage in the active process of being joyful. Evangelical author John Piper provides helpful words regarding this fight:

> Well, God does not mean for us to be passive. He means for us to fight the fight of the faith-the fight for joy. And his central strategy is to preach the gospel to yourself. This is war. Satan is preaching for sure. If we remain passive, we surrender the field to him.[6]

What does Piper mean when he says "preach the gospel to yourself"? This saying could be confusing at first, but I think it provides a deep and rich strategy when it comes to the fight for joy. To preach the gospel to yourself means you actively convince yourself daily of the power of the gospel. At times the gospel will seem foolish to us. Paul realizes this when he writes to the church in Corinth, "For the word of the cross is foolishness to those who are perishing, but it is the power of God to us who are being saved" (1 Corinthians 1:18).

It may seem foolish to forgive your enemies, yet the gospel can set you free to do so. It may seem foolish to deny yourself and take up a cross, yet the gospel gives you the strength, through the Holy Spirit, to do that. It may seem like the most foolish thing in the world to follow Christ, yet the very power of God dwells in those who do.

When we tap into the power of God, we set our hearts on the joy we can find only from a loving Father. We have to fight for this joy and preach this "foolish" gospel to ourselves every day. C. J. Mahaney gives some practical advice with regard to the process of actively preaching the gospel to ourselves. He writes, "Reminding ourselves of the gospel is the most important habit we can establish."[7]

We may not understand the gospel and how it affects our emotions because we do not remind ourselves daily of the gospel. The gospel message is not something we hear at the end of a sermon on a Sunday morning, and it is more than a tract we leave in a bathroom stall. There is more power in the gospel message and the God that it reveals than all the world power and short-lived kingdoms in the history of the world. Many Christians do not understand the implications of the gospel message, nor do they experience its power in their daily lives. Constantly reminding ourselves of the gospel truth is a must for Christians who meditate daily on the promises of God. Reading the scriptures through the worldview of the cross transforms our emotions, our decisions, and, ultimately, the way we look at life.

I wake up every morning and pray a prayer like this: "God I will ruin this day on my own. I need to recall and remember what you have done for me in the gospel through the death, burial, and resurrection of Jesus Christ." This prayer is more than a mantra or a checklist. It's a personal conviction that stems from a personal God who has changed me in incredible ways.

> We may not understand the gospel and how it affects our emotions because we do not remind ourselves daily of the gospel.

Paul Tripp writes, "No one is more influential in your life than you are because no one talks to you more than you do. It's a fact that you and I are in an endless conversation with ourselves."[8] Take a minute to think about this statement; we indeed talk to ourselves more than anyone, and we have more influence on ourselves than we realize. The question we have to answer is simple: is Jesus and his gospel a part of the daily conversation we have with ourselves? Our spiritual growth will move incredibly fast when the gospel moves from a set of principles in which we believe to a message we preach to ourselves daily.

The enemy will have a tough time convincing us of untruth when the preaching of the gospel to ourselves already occupies the pulpit of our hearts. Our ability to preach the gospel to ourselves is linked to how much we will find joy in the day-to-day experience. Why? Because the gospel points us to someone more prominent than what we may experience today. The eternal message of the gospel swallows the temporary experience of life on this earth, even the most devastating experiences. Preaching the gospel is the most effective way to fight for joy.

But this life is not just about us. Paul wrote to the Corinthians, reminding them of this fact: they were not alone. You see, we not only preach the gospel to ourselves, but we are a part of a larger gospel community—the church.

Kevin Wilson

Listen When Others Preach the Gospel to You

A thousand different voices bombard us throughout the day, and not all of their messages are bad. The marketing community works overtime to sell and distribute a thousand different words in an attempt to convince us, the consumers, of the power of the word or the products they are selling. The church in Corinth experienced the same with the different communications during the first century. The people of Corinth had a wide variety of religious messages from which to choose.

David Garland writes about what the Corinthian church faced with the onslaught of different religious messages and worldviews:

> Most persons could accommodate all gods and goddesses into their religious behaviors, and they could choose from a great cafeteria line of religious practices. Many believed that there was safety in numbers: The more gods that one appeased and had on one's side, the better.[9]

The Corinthian church faced some of the same pressures and questions we face today: to which voice will we listen, and which voice will have the most influence on us? The mistake many Christians make is they spend too much time listening to the voices of today and too little time listening to the voice of God.

Paul enters into the conversation with the church at Corinth and offers a gospel-laden insight. He tells the church that he is a worker for their joy. One of Paul's main objectives was for the church to understand the joy they possessed in Christ. The gospel message was not something they only preached to themselves; Paul and others came alongside their faith and preached this gospel message. We need the church to remind us of the one message that strengthens our faith, the gospel of Christ.

> The mistake many Christians make is they spend too much time listening to the voices of today and too little time listening to the voice of God.

As we live life in a community of faith, we remind each other of the most beautiful things—we worship and sing as an example to others around us of the faithfulness of God. We serve and teach as grace enables us to encourage and help one another grow in the faith. Our minds do not have the natural inclination on their own to seek God and the good things he brings.

Paul continually reminded the church to think about the good things of the gospel. He instructed the church, "Whatever is true, whatever is honorable, whatever is just, whatever is pure, whatever is lovely, what is commendable—if there is any moral excellence and if there is anything praiseworthy, dwell on these things" (Philippians 4:8). I don't dwell on things that are honorable, but a faithful friend can remind me of these things. I don't always think about the things that are lovely and pure in my life, but God has given me a local body of believers who remind me to think and dwell on these things. I need others in the church, and the church needs me. We are needed by the church, especially when we have something from the gospel of Christ to share.

We preach the gospel to ourselves first, and then, from the overflow of that, we share with others in our community and the church. Why? Because we need to stand firm in our faith. Our world needs to see the power of the gospel through the faithful lives of those who are the redeemed of Christ.

One of the things we say in my church is that we want to be known more for what we are *for* than what we are *against*. Our communities may not have a favorable opinion of the church because we have had a message of condemnation instead of the message of the gospel. The more we preach the life-changing, life-giving gospel of Jesus to ourselves and others, the more joy we will have in our hearts to face each day and share the message of hope Jesus has given us. So, friend, fight for joy. Fight hard, and fight for others to experience the joy we all can find in Christ.

Questions for Personal Reflection

1. How do you fight for joy?
2. What tends to steal your joy?
3. Do you hear counsel well? Why or why not?

CHAPTER 19
Finding Joy in Suffering

Keeping our eyes on Jesus, the source and perfecter of our faith. For the joy that lay before him, he endured the cross, despising the shame, and sat down at the right hand of the throne of God.
—Hebrews 12:2

One of the joys I have experienced as a parent is receiving homemade gifts from my children. I have a couple of shoeboxes full of letters, crafts, and oddly shaped clay knickknacks dedicated to me as a father. One gift I have loved receiving is the annual Christmas ornament. The other day my daughter presented me with the ornament she made during her fourth-grade year. The ornament displayed the word JOY, with the O containing a picture of her beautiful face. The gift was hand-painted and very well done, and it occupies a space on our Christmas tree, along with many other handmade gifts from over the years. When I look at this small gift, I experience so many different emotions. I feel proud, thankful, peaceful, and, most of all, joyful.

When I look at this ornament, however, I can't say that the word *suffering* occupies my thoughts. Most of us do not connect the word joy with the word suffering. How can pain have any correlation with joy? How can an excruciating experience produce joy in our lives? Usually, we want to keep suffering out of our lives; it's something we do not want to experience, even though we know we will. At the cross of Jesus, however, joy and suffering meet in a divine dance, producing

> At the cross of Jesus, however, joy and suffering meet in a divine dance, producing justification and forgiveness for sinners.

justification and forgiveness for sinners. To fully understand joy, we have to walk through the fire of affliction.

Cross-Eyed Vision

The book of Hebrews is a complex book that can awaken the soul to the beauty of God's love found in the Old Testament and the glorious new life we see in Jesus Christ. The writer of Hebrews opens chapter 12 by setting the example and work of Jesus as the apex of God's work here on earth. The author instructs his readers to "keep their eyes on Jesus." Often, this is one of our most challenging tasks. It's difficult because we usually keep our eyes on our performances instead of the finished work of Jesus.

Ask yourself an important question: *who or what has my attention?* What motivates you or hinders your spiritual growth? Many have their eyes focused on a particular person, and their joy and passion for life ebbs and flows in correlation with how they relate to that person or how that person is performing. Remember, your ability to experience real joy is dependent upon what or who you choose to attach joy. If you are always looking at another's performance for your happiness and motivation, then you will experience disappointment at some time.

Some people blame their lack of joy on others. They tell themselves they would have been happier if their parents had raised them differently, or they think if their supervisor, teacher, or coach would see their potential, then they would experience more joy.

We tend to have high expectations for the things and people in our lives to produce joy.

We even place these expectations on ourselves; we may expect our talents, intellect, and skills to bring us the joy we believe we deserve. Remember that emotions are not bad, but when emotions rule us, we tend to not honor God with our actions and hearts. For example, God allowed me to be a student pastor for many years, and during this time, I was able to have an ongoing dialogue with many high school students as they prepared for college and life beyond adolescence. One of the things I observed was the amount of pressure the students placed on themselves to

> We tend to have high expectations for the things and people in our lives to produce joy.

perform. This pressure was applied in their athletic, academic, and spiritual lives. I watched many lose their joy when they did not perform well in one of these categories.

The saddest for me to watch was when a student struggled spiritually. Their entire lives might take a tragic turn because they had identified themselves with their abilities to keep the law and prove themselves to God. Again and again, I saw well-meaning, faithful people lose their happiness due to their lack of "cross-eyed vision."

Cross-eyed vision is the ability to focus on the power of the cross, instead of our ability to keep us in right standing with God.

Again, legalism can rear its ugly head when we base our spirituality on our ability to perform, instead of on Christ's sufficient, substitutionary, atoning sacrifice on the cross. This truth is why the writer of Hebrews instructs us to keep our eyes on Jesus as the "source and perfecter of our faith." The writer does not mean for us to ignore others who have helped our faith or brought joy into our life, as God uses a wide variety of experiences and people to help us grow in Christ.

> Cross-eyed vision is the ability to focus on the power of the cross, instead of our ability to keep us in right standing with God.

The apostle Paul understood this truth when he wrote,

> But speaking the truth in love, let us grow in every way into him who is the head-Christ. From him the whole body, fitted and knit together by every supporting ligament, promotes the growth of the body for building up itself in love by the proper working of each individual part. (Ephesians 4:15–16)

There is a beautifully divine dance as God uses different people and experiences to promote the growth of the body. But this growth is all in Christ, and we all "grow in every way into him"; this is why the writer of Hebrews can say that Christ is the source of all spiritual growth and joy in a person's life.

Not only is he the source, but he is the perfecter. I have told my kids, over and over, "You are not perfect; only Jesus is perfect." I often have to remind myself of these words as well. We find this useful as a family because our default setting is to place way too much responsibility for success on our shoulders. I don't mean only spiritual success; I mean accomplishment in any area of life. We will be very disappointed if we believe we are the key to perfecting the power of change in our or anyone else's life.

One of the many reasons we are not the key to perfecting love and power is that we are weak and fragile. Our lives can't bear the full weight of a perfect life before God. We will all fail at one point or another, but when we admit we are weak and we fix our eyes on Jesus, a great amount of joy can be experienced, despite our efforts.

Paul Tripp writes the following concerning weakness: "Weakness demonstrates what has been true all along: we are completely dependent on God for life and breath and everything else. Weakness was not the end for me, but a new beginning."[10] Tripp wrote these words on the heels of an incredible time of suffering. Our ability to fix our eyes on Jesus as we endure the reality of our weakness opens the door to suffering well and not losing our joy when hard things come our way—and like it or not, hard things will happen.

Finding Joy in the Suffering of Jesus

The search for joy is a difficult journey, and many of us have to fight daily for this elusive emotion. The author of Hebrews uses the word *joy* to describe how Jesus approached the cross. Think about what brings you joy. Is it an experience, a person, or a place? Is it a quiet morning away from the pressures of life? Is it a good book or a to-do list with all the boxes checked? Do you find joy when everyone around you has kept their promises and treated you fairly? Most of us would find some satisfaction or joy when we see one or all of the above in our lives. Most of us find joy when our lives are headed in the right direction; although generalized, that statement is, for the most part, true.

We find joy when we gain something, not lose something. This is where the approach of Jesus to the cross confounds us. He approaches the cross "for the joy that lay before him." The words of Jon Stott help us understand Jesus's motivation: "What dominated his mind was not the living but the giving of his life."[11] Jesus knew that the cross meant total separation from his Father, a breaking of the relationship he had known from before time in the annals of eternity past, yet he endured the pain of the wrath of God and the cup of his judgment against sin to purchase his children from their sin. The cross allows the people of God to live in joy and peace before the Father. The cross is where the shame of sin is resolved, and the people of God can experience the treasure of God himself. *The cross is where Jesus experienced the greatest suffering and the greatest joy.*

Most of us probably are familiar with the suffering Jesus experienced on the cross—his suffering has been displayed in books, plays, and even movies. The scriptures paint a vivid picture of the suffering of Jesus.

> He was despised and rejected by men, a man of suffering who knew what sickness was. He was like someone people turned away from, he was despised, and we didn't value him. Yet he himself bore our sicknesses, and he carried our pains; but we in turn regarded him stricken, struck down by God, and afflicted. (Isaiah 53:3–4)

We may be a little more familiar with the suffering experienced at the cross. The writer of Hebrews describes Jesus as the one who "endured the cross, despising the shame." The enduring work and suffering of the cross were costly for our Lord, not only his life but for the separation from his Father and the pain of the wrath of God. Suffering is not the only thing experienced in the atoning sacrifice of Jesus. The cross paved a way back for us, back to the throne, back to a right relationship with the Lord. There was a seat that needed to be occupied in heaven, and no grave would keep the rightful King from occupying it!

In the greatest suffering, Jesus was given the right to sit at the right hand of God the Father, interceding on behalf for his church for all eternity, until every last one of us dines with him in his kingdom.

So we can suffer well, and we don't have to lose our joy in the midst of our trials. I don't look forward to these trials, but I do know they are working something beautiful and joyful in me—a joy that is only experienced in the dark times of life. My wife and I have a dear friend who has suffered much. She has endured more heartache and loss than I may ever experience. We were walking together and talking about the situation and how it is shaping and affecting her life. We talked about the emotions she was wrestling with and how Jesus was holding her during this time.

As we talked, God brought a section of scripture to our minds. In 2 Corinthians 4:17–18, Paul writes, "For our momentary light affliction is producing for us an absolutely incomparable eternal weight of glory. So we do not focus on what is seen, but what is unseen." As we ended our walk, I was so heartbroken for my friend's suffering but so full of joy for what God was doing in her life. Her "momentary light affliction" was producing a joy that can only be forged in the crucible of suffering.

If you are experiencing suffering, don't fix your eyes on anything but Jesus, for he occupies a sovereign throne in heaven, and he sees your suffering and can produce joy in your life, not only in spite of your suffering but through your suffering.

Questions for Personal Reflection

1. How has Jesus met you in your suffering?
2. What causes you the most suffering in this life?
3. What does it mean to have a "cross-eyed" vision?

deep down in the depths of my heart.

CHAPTER 20
Rooted in Joy

And the seed on the rock are those who, when they hear, receive the word with joy. Having no root, these believe for a while and fall away at a time of testing.
—Luke 8:13

One of the significant aspects of joy we have expressed is that happiness is attached to someone or something. We may think the best way to be joyful is to connect our joy to something that can stand the test of time. Indeed, this is partly true. Christians have found an inexhaustible amount of joy in God. Psalm 16:11 states, "You reveal the path of life to me; in your presence is abundant joy; at your right hand are eternal pleasures."

In chapter 19, we saw that after Jesus endured the suffering of the cross, he sat down at the right hand of God. What an incredible thought this is—in Christ, we have everything we need from God. Jesus is the one who ushers his children into the presence of the Father, where we find abundant joy and eternal pleasures. No other worldview or religion gives complete access to the heavenly Father and the enjoyment he offers.

Some may not believe we can find God or that God even exists, yet they desire joy. So the most rational option would be to seek out activities, a lifestyle, people, places, and things that can bring the most joy for the longest time. This approach, however, could be in vain. As I've mentioned, connecting our joy to something that stands the test of time is only half of the equation. Experiencing the complete joy Jesus wants for us is found at the foot of the cross in the presence of God. The question becomes, does it satisfy us enough to stay there?

Kevin Wilson

Loving Him Enough to Stay

In Luke 8, we see Jesus teaching the parable of the four soils to his disciples. He says the seed is the word of God, and the four "soils" are how the word of God is received, with the last soil accepting the seed long enough to germinate and produce fruit. How does this parable help us understand true joy? Verse thirteen states, "When they hear, receive the word with joy." Here, Jesus attaches joy to our receiving the Word of God.

Paul writes in Romans 10:14, "How then, can they call on him they have not believed in? And how can they believe without hearing about him?" Paul is saying the preaching of the Word is how conversion and faith occur. As we faithfully minister the Word of God to those in our circles of influence, God will speak to their hearts, convict them of sin and the judgment to come, and give the grace needed to respond to the gospel message.

For thousands of years, humans have responded to the effectual call of God upon their lives. But what about when we see emotional decisions that seem not to last the test of time. I have seen several people receive the Word with joy, but they don't last very long in the faith. Do they lose their faith? No, when God is the author and perfecter of our faith, it's not ours to lose. My church has taught a saying, "Once saved, always saved." This is helpful but often misleading. This mantra can lead people to pray a prayer, or sign a card, or make a profession of faith through baptism, thinking true conversion has happened, when indeed it has not.

Theologian and pastor J. D. Greear has helpful words regarding salvation and genuine faith: "Salvation is not a prayer you pray in a one-time ceremony and then move on from; salvation is a posture of repentance and faith that you begin in a moment and maintain for the rest of your life."[12] This posture of repentance and faith are continually renewed in Christ as we abide in his grace. Hence, we do not lose our salvation, and we are once saved, always persevering. The people who believe with joy and then falls away has a root problem. Their joy was found at first in an emotional, spiritual experience, but it did not stand the test of time. Hence, it was never rooted in Jesus.

We are not perfect, and we do sin. The believer must always stand guard against the temptation of the enemy and the onslaught of culture and the world. He or she will fall and often fail, but God will restore and hold the believer fast.

One of the most powerful pictures of grace is seen in the Old Testament book of Hosea. Hosea, a prophet of God, is told to marry a prostitute named Gomer, have children with her, watch her run back to her lovers, and then repurchase her. God is using the picture of Hosea and Gomer as a snapshot of the love he has for his people. God doesn't only *allow* his people to come back; he earnestly yearns for them to come to him. Hosea 2:14 says, "I am going to persuade her, lead her to the wilderness and speak tenderly to her."

God says he will persuade his people to come back to him by speaking tender words over them. He will bring hope to the hopeless and peace to situations where there is not peace. The gospel message lures prodigal sons and daughters, prostitutes, thieves, and every other sinner home from the pigpen and back to the waiting arms of the Father, who loves them unconditionally. A thousand times over, we will repent of our sins and fall on the grace that brought us to him in the first place. True conversion can be emotional, but a lasting mark of true faith is seen in the perseverance of the one claiming faith. Those whom God calls, he keeps.

> The gospel message lures prodigal sons and daughters, prostitutes, thieves, and every other sinner home from the pigpen and back to the waiting arms of the Father, who loves them unconditionally.

The Permanence of God's Love

There is a permanence to the effectual call of God to salvation. We do not have to worry if God will get tired of holding us in his strong right hand. God's love and salvation are fixed and unchanging, and this produces the greatest joy. This joy stands the test of time and the testing of our faith. Genuine faith is a bulwark against our fickle and ever-changing emotions and attitudes. The permanence of this salvation is an essential aspect of our relationship to God and relationships in general. Many Christians do not experience the joy they have in Christ because they believe God is ready to give up on them after one mistake, one mishap, and one fall along the path. This statement is not meant to minimize sin. Sin is more than a mistake, a failing, or a mishap. It takes the applied blood of the slain sacrificial Lamb to take away the sins of the world.

We walk in the beauty of the resurrected Lord, free from the condemnation and the guilt of the world. We see truth echoed in the words of Romans 8, a chapter Derek W. H. Thomas calls "the best chapter in the Bible."[13] Romans 8 begins with these words: "Therefore, there is now no condemnation for those in Christ Jesus." Christ deals with our sin at the cross and destroys the condemnation caused by our rebellions against God.

Understanding the finished work of Jesus upon the cross is one of the most liberating truths we can uncover on this spiritual pilgrimage. The finished work of Jesus allows the permanence of the relationships we have to blossom in incredible joy. This truth is one of the most practical tools we can carry into our everyday lives, especially when it comes to our vertical and horizontal relationships. Our horizontal relationships can be permanent because of the established and permanent relationship we have with the Father in Christ. Because of the gospel, we don't run out on our kids, our spouses, our families, or our church.

Timothy Keller reflects upon the gospel and the staying power of God with these words:

> Well, when Jesus looked down from the cross, he didn't think "I am giving myself to you because you are attractive to me." No, he was in agony, and he looked down at us-denying him, abandoning him, and betraying him-and in the greatest act of love in history, he STAYED.[14]

> *Understanding the finished work of Jesus upon the cross is one of the most liberating truths we can uncover on this spiritual pilgrimage.*

We continue in the relationships he gave us with joy because he stayed when we were in the depths of our sins. We remain long when the night is dark and the landscape is barren and wild. We remain in the good and the bad because God never denies his children, nor does he hold his love for ransom. The abiding relationship we have with Jesus is what roots our joy and makes it complete. The Holy Spirit will awaken our hearts every day to this one reality: Jesus is the only place we find real happiness.

Questions for Personal Reflection

1. How does the gospel encourage you to continue in the faith?
2. What emotions are awakened when you think about the permanence of God's love?
3. What affections are awakened when you think about Christ enduring the cross for you?

CHAPTER 21
When Grief Shows Up

> Then Martha said to Jesus "Lord, if you had been here, my brother wouldn't have died. Yet even now I know that whatever you ask from God, God will give you."
> —John 11:21–22

Grief will show up on your doorstep at one time or another, and death will not always be the delivery man. We can grieve several experiences in our lives. The loss of a relationship, the choices our adult children make, the lost opportunity or the promotion that passed us over—these may well cause our hearts to grieve. The emotion of grief is one of the most powerful that we will experience in our lifetimes. Notice it's not a matter of *if* we will experience grief; we *will* experience grief. There is a silver lining to the darkness of grief, however, that we will explore in the following chapters.

When Grief Knocks at Your Door

I can recall the early morning moments of March 3, 1999, very well. It's hard to remember the events of just a typical day from the past, but this day was far from ordinary. On this day, my older sister passed away due to a drug overdose. My sister and I were very close when I was in elementary school; she was twelve years older than me, so she was assigned the task of looking after me, the youngest in the family. On summer days, we would swim in our pool until the evening hours. She married when I was nine and moved into a small double-wide on an acre of land, nestled behind our parents' home. The early part of her marriage was uneventful. She gave birth to a son, the first grandchild in our family, and began her new life with her husband and child, but over the years, sin crept into their lives as she began to change.

The changes were subtle at first—sleeping in on the weekends until the early afternoon hours, not showing up for family events, and other abnormal behavior. Slowly, our family noticed other changes to her moral character. My parents caught her stealing money and lying to cover up her actions. Over the years, she had become addicted to methamphetamine, or "meth." The drug is highly addictive, and without intervention, users' lives usually end horribly. I watched my parents, who are believers, support and love her despite her addiction, but in the early hours of March 3, 1999, she died of an overdose.

That year I was away at college, so my parents called the church I was attending, and one of the pastors drove to my apartment to break the news of my sister's passing. When I heard the story, I was shocked but not surprised. I can still envision the bathroom where I was standing when I heard the knock on the door, and Bill, the pastor who broke the news, asked if he could talk to me. *Grief has a way of amplifying every part of a situation.*

Almost twenty years have passed since my sister died, and time has healed so much, but I can still feel the sting of what could have been. She never attended my wedding, never knew my wife or children; they only know her from family pictures and stories I tell. Grief has a way of stealing the moments in our lives and replacing them with the reality of living in a broken world.

> Grief has a way of amplifying every part of a situation.

In John 11, Mary and Martha experience the existence of a broken world. John 11 starts with these words: "Now a man was sick, Lazarus from Bethany, the village of Mary and her sister Martha." John does not give us the reason why Lazarus was sick, but we are given a few important details.

- Mary was the one who anointed the Lord with perfume and wiped his feet with her hair.
- Jesus heard about the sickness before Lazarus died.
- Jesus loved Mary, Martha, and Lazarus.

The last detail listed above is an important one. Jesus loved everyone who was affected by the imminent death of Lazarus. More amazing are the words Jesus spoke when he found out about the condition of this man he knew and loved.

> This sickness will not end in death but is for the glory of God, so that the Son of God may be glorified through it. (John 11:4)

Notice Jesus said "sickness will not end in death." God doesn't promise his children a life far from the effects of death, sin, and the fall, but he does promise a better ending. Often, the effects cloud the promise of a better ending.

C. S. Lewis said that the view we have in a broken world is one of being "on the wrong side of the door."[15] The wrong side of the door is a scary place; we don't know what is coming up, and fear and anxiety can grip our hearts, shaping the emotions we experience. Yet the words of Jesus give us the eternal perspective needed. God can take moments filled with grief and show his children the glory of God within those moments, not outside of those moments. God doesn't need to change what is happening; he can hold you through your grief and use it to shape you with his gospel.

> God doesn't promise his children a life far from the effects of death, sin, and the fall, but he does promise a better ending.

Martha's reaction is twofold. First, she struggles to align what she knows to be true—that Jesus loves her—with his tardiness. She laments, "Lord if you had been here, my brother wouldn't have died." One can hear the grief in her voice. John 11:6 states that upon hearing of his friend's sickness, Jesus stayed two more days in the place where he was. John 10 puts Jesus's location on the eastern side of the Jordan River, maybe a day's walk from the village of Bethany. Why did Jesus tarry? Why didn't he come when he heard of his friend's condition? It is possible Martha struggled with the same questions that we do when God doesn't seem to answer our despair. The "Where are you, God?" question is one people have struggled with through the years.

David begins Psalm 13 with the following: "How long Lord? Will you forget me forever?" The prophet Habakkuk writes, "How long, LORD, must I call for help and you do not listen" (Habakkuk 1:2). We see a similar passionate plea when those who gave their lives for the faith cried out to God for justice: "They cried out with a loud voice: 'Lord, the one who is holy and true, how long until you judge those who live on the earth and avenge our blood?'" (Revelation 6:10).

At one point or another, we all question God's timing, especially when our hearts are squeezed by grief. During these times, we will hold on to our convictions about the nature of God, or we will allow our circumstances to dictate who we believe God to be at the moment of our grief.

Everyone is a theologian, but not everyone is a *good* theologian. We all have thoughts about God—how he should act and reply to the problems that occur in the world, how he should answer when we call, and especially the timing of his answer. Martha had a dead brother and a tardy Lord, and this did not compute with her. Still, even in her grief, she does acknowledge the overall sovereignty of Jesus, especially the relationship he has with the Father.

The second reaction we see from Martha centers on her acknowledgment that Jesus is still in control. John 11:22 states, "Yet even now I know that whatever you ask from God, God will give you." Such great faith! Her brother is dead, and she still can see the power of the Son of God standing before her. Remember, grief puts us on the "wrong side of the door." While we occupy this earthly home, we will not be immune to hurt and pain. Creation is groaning from the effects of the fall of man, and as Paul said, "The whole creation has been groaning together with labor pains until now ... we also groan within ourselves, eagerly waiting for adoption, the redemption of our bodies" (Romans 8:22–23). Paul stated in theological terms what Martha experienced on this temporal plane.

We yearn for God to make everything better, to redeem the hard things in our lives, and to make something useful from our grief. Martha understood that while she felt the sting of grief and death, one stood before her who could do something about it. But Jesus wants us to see something that goes beyond our grief. He desires for his children to see him not only as the comforter and the one in control but the one who is life itself.

We see the power of the gospel in the reaction and dialogue Jesus has with Martha. Jesus tells her, "Your brother will rise again" (John 11:23). This amazing statement is one that should have dispelled her grief, yet Martha does not catch the reality of Jesus's words. She answers Jesus, "I know that he will rise again in the resurrection as the last day" (John 11:24). Martha believed in the resurrection, but just the resurrection of the last day, not today.

We say to those who are grieving, "Time will heal your heart." But what about the grace we need for the present? Martha had given up on her situation. She had come to grips with the death of her brother, and it never occurred to her why Jesus was standing in front of her. Maybe he came to the town to comfort his friends or to pay his final respects. In reality, he came because he is King over death. Jesus did not come only to comfort those who grieve; he also came to give hope to those who mourn. And in the case of Martha and Mary, he would not wait until the last day. Hope happened on this day.

God doesn't always take our grief away quickly, but the truth we find in John 11:25–26 is what every grieving heart needs to hear and believe: "Jesus said to her, 'I am the resurrection and the life. The one who believes in me, even if he dies, will live.'" Jesus's words are the key to the gospel's radically transforming the way we live and the way we approach grief. Death only held the decaying body of Lazarus because Jesus allowed it. There is life and power in the name of Jesus but also in what Jesus declares. Jesus plainly said, "Lazarus, come forth," and death and decay had to let him go.

> Death only held the decaying body of Lazarus because Jesus allowed it.

Our grief may not always be fixed, but it can bow at the feet of Jesus. The reality and dynamic of this family changed with one word from Jesus. Jesus may not change our circumstances, but his cross and gospel radically change our perspectives.

I still grieve my sister, and I have lost others since her death. But I do not grieve as one who has no hope. Because of the sin and decay of this world, I will experience grief again, but it does not have to shape who I am. I know the one who has conquered everything, who brings me grief and pain, so I lay my grief at his nail-pierced feet.

> I know the one who has conquered everything, who brings me grief and pain, so I lay my grief at his nail-pierced feet.

Questions for Personal Reflection

1. How has grief amplified a situation in your life?
2. What are you grieving in your life currently?
3. What does the cross mean to those who are grieving?

CHAPTER 22
The Grief of Loss

Then the word of the LORD came to me: "Son of man, I am about to take the delight of your eyes away from you with a fatal blow."
—Ezekiel 24:15–16

Grief will show itself in a variety of different ways. Psychologists have identified that people go through five different stages of grief. David Kessler identifies these stages as "denial, anger, bargaining, depression, and acceptance."[16] These stages were first developed by Elisabeth Kübler-Ross in her 1969 book *On Death and Dying*. Sometimes the lines get blurred between these stages, but these are the common ways grief will express itself. The topic of grief has launched countless books and seminars to help people deal with this difficult emotion. Certified grief counselors are trained to help people navigate these tricky waters.

Most grief deals with a loss of some kind—the kind of loss that takes our breath away; the type of loss that seems so permanent that no amount of searching will recover it. Concerning this idea of loss, C. S. Lewis said, "How often-will it be for always?-how often will the vast emptiness astonish me like a complete novelty and make me say 'I never realized my loss till this moment'? The same leg is cut off time after time."[17]

Grief often feels this way. This emotion has a way of coming back stronger with each passing phase. Time will heal, but time will not let us forget what or who we have lost. Grief is not something we will ever get used to, but it is something we can get through.

Kevin Wilson

The Shocking Pain of Loss

The prophet Ezekiel is a portrait of God's grace during a difficult season of grief and loss. Ezekiel is one of the first prophets to speak to Israel outside of the Promised Land. Ezekiel was a priest, and he heard the word of the Lord during the exile of God's people.

> While I was among the exiles by the Chebar Canel, the heavens were opened, and I saw visions of God. (Ezekiel 1:1)

Ezekiel had already known heartache. Born within the borders of Israel and then having lived around five years in the Chebar Canel, the prophet only had memories of his time living within the Promised Land. The Babylonians deported many from Jerusalem in 598 BC. Ezekiel had lost his homeland, but in the midst of this loss, God spoke to him. Ezekiel's circumstances remind us that God is not bound or limited by where or in what circumstances we find ourselves; he speaks and acts outside of our current situation. Ezekiel continued to hear the "word of the LORD" throughout his time in exile.

Grief can feel like an exile. Everything changes; nothing is the same. We speak familiar words into empty places, and the emptiness reminds us of that which we have lost. Grief seems to bring out particular suffering in our lives. We often wonder, *When will this suffering end?* The walls of pain and loss seem to close in around us as we sort out the hand we've been dealt. Ezekiel 24 gives us a gospel-shaped view of grief, a view that, although painful, does not hinder our growth or our identities. In Ezekiel 24:16, Ezekiel is informed that God will take away the "delight of your eyes." This revelation of the "word of the LORD" is followed by one of the most staggering verses in the Bible.

> God is not bound or limited by where or in what circumstances we find ourselves; he speaks and acts outside of our current situation.

Ezekiel 24:18 states: "I spoke to the people in the morning, and my wife died in the evening." The light of his eyes was indeed snuffed out as Ezekiel suffered the loss of his wife. The shocking news of this incident was not in the loss of a spouse. As painful as that sounds, people experience the deaths of spouses each day—some expected and some unexpected. No, the shocking part of this story is God's response to Ezekiel's circumstance.

> Groan quietly; do not observe mourning rites for the dead. Put on your turban and strap sandals on your feet. (Ezekiel 24:17)

At first glance, the response of the Lord seems cruel and uncaring, but there is a purpose in what the prophet is experiencing. Only the gospel brings out this purpose and offers hope to those in the midst of suffering. The gospel worldview is the only belief system that can make sense out of grief and loss.

Tim Keller explains with the following words: "While other worldviews lead us to sit in the midst of life's joys, foreseeing the coming sorrows, Christianity empowers its people to sit in the midst of the world's sorrows, tasting the coming joy."[18] Only the believer who has his identity in God alone can face the sorrows of the world, while also looking forward to the coming joy. The gospel message of Jesus allows us to meet grief while putting on our turbans and obediently following God. The gospel message helps people understand suffering and grief in the world by showing us a Father who willing gives his Son as a sacrifice for his children, but it also empowers us to go through our gardens of agony. Whether we suffer the loss of a spouse, a sister, or other people things we hold dear, the gospel gives us hope along the way.

C. S. Lewis said the following regarding the loss of a spouse: "The death of a beloved is an amputation."[19] Indeed, this is what the Word of the Lord felt like when it came to the prophet. The prophet was able to obey God while walking through this difficult circumstance.

They Will Know I Am God

We see the reasoning behind the death of Ezekiel's spouse: "Now Ezekiel will be a sign for you. You will do everything he has done. When this happens, you will know that I am the LORD God" (Ezekiel 24:24). What would happen? God would take the "delight of Israel's eyes away." He would take away their sanctuary. He would take away his presence, and he would take away his protection. Israel had wandered far from God, but to Israel, it did not feel that far from God. Israel had become very talented in incorporating the rituals and practices of the pagan people around them into the life of their faith. They had lost their first love and forgotten the Lord, who alone did great things for them. Like an unruly schoolchild, Israel was going to be disciplined by God.

At first glance, the Lord seems cruel and harsh, yet God is unchanging in his character and attributes, as well as in his love for his people. God knows he is the only one who can satisfy our hearts' longings. The people of Israel allowed their sin to satisfy their craving for life. Sin only brings death. There is not living in sin; this is one of the chief lies of the enemy. He tricks us into thinking sin will satisfy long term, but this is not true. Sin leads us on a path away from the joy of God and into the stronghold of death. Jesus, the author and giver of life, gave his life for his beloved so we could enjoy the satisfaction of a relationship with Father, but we may choose sin instead of God.

Praise God that he intervenes with the gospel, pointing us back to the correct understanding that he is God, and none other can satisfy. John Piper has stated, "I know of no other way to triumph over sin long-term than to gain a distaste for it because of a superior satisfaction in God."[20] Piper stated a truth that we, as believers, should embrace daily in our lives. Namely, sin will never satisfy as God can satisfy. Sin will never provide as God can provide. Sin will never give us life; sin only brings death.

Ezekiel was to be a sign to the people of Israel. A sign that pointed them back to the beauty of God; it was a reminder to forsake their ways and embrace the beauty of God. God paved his will for Ezekiel with the bricks of grief. And so parts of our stories will be paved with the same bricks. We will experience grief in this life. Sometimes grief will come upon us suddenly; sometimes we will experience grief in a seemingly never-ending cycle. The one thing we can trust is that God will be with us in the middle of our grief.

The gospel does not depict a God who is far away from the suffering of this world. He has not pardoned himself from the grief that sin has brought upon his creation. Isaiah 53:4–5 gives us a glimpse of how God heals our grief:

Yet he himself bore our sicknesses, and he carried our pains; but we in turn regarded him stricken, struck down by God, and afflicted. But he was pierced because of our rebellion, crushed because of our iniquities; punishment for our peace was on him, and we are healed by his wounds.

We can have hope in the midst of our suffering and grief because Jesus experienced far greater pain than even the loss of a loved one brings. When we experience grief, we do so in the presence of God. We are not cast out of his presence just because we are going through a difficult time. Jesus experienced the full wrath of God, not because of anything he did but because of what we did. We have all turned toward the delights of this world, forsaking our Creator. And we all deserve the wrath of God, yet we do not have to die. Someone died in our place, someone upon whom the sins of the world were laid as a sacrificial Lamb, taking away our sin and our impurities and allowing us to walk with God in actual life. This way of living is the only way we know that the Lord is God.

We only experience the joy of God through the death of Christ. Our joy and life are given to us freely because Jesus gave his life willingly. There is no other way to experience eternal life but through the cross of Christ.

Maybe the path you are walking is paved with the same bricks of grief as Ezekiel's path. Perhaps not today but someday, we will all walk this path, one of hurt, confusion, pain, and grief. But we can have confidence in this one thing: we do not walk alone, and we do not experience the full weight of grief. Jesus has taken our grief and walked our paths, and he has given us everything we need to get through this life, even when grief shows up. So pray to him, fall on him, run to him in the midst of grief. He is the shining light!

> We only experience the joy of God through the death of Christ.

Questions for Personal Reflection

1. How do you deal with loss?
2. What is the hardest item/relationship you have lost?
3. How does it feel when you experience a personal loss?

CHAPTER 23
The Grief Over Sin

Completely wash away my guilt and cleanse me from sin. For I am conscious of my rebellion, and my sin is always before me. Against you–you alone–I have sinned and done this evil in your sight. So you are right when you pass sentence; you are blameless when you judge.
—Psalm 51:2–4

Sin never keeps its promises. Sin will promise pleasure, life, and joy but will never hold up its end of the bargain. Sin will drag our hearts away from our Creator and Lord quicker than anything else in this world. The consequences of sin will often last a lifetime. The nature of sin is all-consuming; like fire, it doesn't stop when pain is felt or loss is experienced. We struggle with it every day.

Sin has caused me more grief than anything else in my life. The problem is, I grieved more over the consequences of my sin than the sin itself. I've said that grief is one of those emotions we don't care to experience. As previously mentioned, we associate grief with loss or an emotional upheaval of some sort. Grief is not a pleasant experience, yet grieving over our sins can be one of the most freeing and spiritual-growth moments in our lives. What does it mean to mourn our sin? King David gives us an excellent picture of what true repentance and remorse looks like in the life of a believer.

Do You Mortify?

John Owen, a great Puritan pastor and theologian in the seventeenth century, wrote the following regarding the believer's attitude toward sin:

"Do you mortify? Do you make it your daily work? Be always at it whilst you live; cease not a day from this work; be killing sin or it is killing you."[21] We may not be familiar with the word choice Mr. Owen used to describe the believer's attitude toward sin. He encouraged the family of God to make it their daily habit to "mortify" the sin that so easily can entangle their lives, but in today's Christian circles, this is not a word that occupies our conversations. It's not a trendy word used to describe a Christian bestseller. You will not find this word as a lyric in a catchy worship-and-praise chorus or even a popular hymn. Owen believed dying to self and sin must happen daily in the life of a believer. Can you feel the tension? Killing sin is not something we make a habit of talking about, yet according to Owen, we should kill sin, or it will kill us. What is he talking about?

Certainly, some sins are harmful and will take our or another's life, but those are not the sins with which most of us wrestle. We have a "stair-step theology" when it comes to sin. We order the severity of sin much like a set of stairs, with the most dangerous ones ascending in order—usually, the ones we deem the more serious sins are the ones with which we do not struggle. Those sins—the more dangerous ones—are for the "other" people, those who are immoral and vile.

Our language has changed dramatically over the years when we speak of sin—if we address sin at all. Sin is reduced to a wrong turn, a mistake, or a bad choice. Hanging in my house is a sign reading, "God sees me, and he understands." This is the motto of the day. God sees my actions, and he understands that I sin, and he will forgive me. We expect others to forgive us as well. We think our choices and actions do not have consequences attached to them. I have watched as couples have made "mistakes" and then are so amazed when the consequences of these mistakes are more than they can stand.

We play with the poisonous snake of sin and are surprised when it strikes and takes our lives. Part of the modern-day struggles with sin is seen in the way Christians have approached the way we deal with sin. Many see the cure for sin as being behavior modification and moral living. This is not the picture that scripture paints of sin or how to take care of sin.

Sin Is More than a Behavioral Problem; It's a Heart Problem

Sin is so much more than a behavioral problem; it's a heart problem. Sin is not like a bruise on an apple or a little mold on your bread. It's not like a nonmalignant tumor that can be taken out with surgery. Sin is invasive and all-consuming, and we will never grieve sin until we start at a heart level.

The Bible does not reduce sin to something behavioral alone. Sin does present itself in actions, attitudes, and behaviors, but this is the only the tip of the iceberg. Sin goes deep into the heart of humanity, making us rotten to the core. The prophet Jeremiah understood how sin affected our hearts when he wrote, "The heart is more deceitful than anything else, and incurable-who can understand it?" (Jeremiah 17:9). Jeremiah addressed what every human being struggles with; namely, a heart that is wicked, deceitful, and rebellious against a good God.

> Sin is invasive and all-consuming, and we will never grieve sin until we start at a heart level.

Sin goes so much further than our actions; our motives and hearts are parts of the equation. That's why more than our behavior has to change. Our hearts have to turn, and then our actions and choices will follow. Our hearts do not want to follow the commands and decrees of a holy God naturally. We all have renegade hearts—hearts that want to declare mutiny against the God of heaven. How do you tame a renegade heart?

> We all have renegade hearts—hearts that want to declare mutiny against the God of heaven.

Grieving Our Begins with Godly Sorrow

Paul wrote, "For godly grief produces a repentance that leads to salvation without regret, but worldly grief produces death" (2 Corinthians 7:10). Before we will ever have victory over the day-to-day sin that entangles our lives, we must understand the difference between worldly grief and the godly sorrow that leads to repentance. Before we ever put to the death the sin that is trying to choke the life out of us, we must learn what Paul refers to in Romans 8.

> If you live according to the flesh, you are going to die. But if by the Spirit you put to death the deeds of the body, you will live. (Romans 8:13)

The Holy Spirit of God that indwells every child of God will point out the sin in our lives that we need to mortify. Every day, the children of God need to ask the following question of the Holy Spirit: "What part of me needs to die today?" We will never ask this question if we feel comfortable with our sins. Feeling comfortable with our sins is a sign of worldly sorrow. We may not like our sins, we may think they are bad, we may even see that they affect our relationship with God, but we still keep them around. We may distance ourselves from them and lock them in the cellar or the attic of our lives, but they still live and breathe and have control of us.

John Owen was right: "Be killing sin, or it will be killing you." Godly grief and sorrow can help us here. Godly sorrow brings repentance. One of the jobs of the Holy Spirit is to show us our sin, convict us of our sin, and point us to Jesus, who can take care of our sin.

> Every day, the children of God need to ask the following question of the Holy Spirit: "What part of me needs to die today?"

John wrote the following concerning the role of the Holy Spirit: "When he comes, he will convict the world about sin, righteousness, and judgment" (John 16:8). As we abide with Christ, the Holy Spirit convicts us of our sin and allows us to grieve our sin with a godly sorrow that leads to repentance and full restoration with God. Worldly sorrow and grief—just feeling sorry or sad for a mistake or a bad judgment—only leads to death. Call sin what it is. It's more than a mistake or a bad choice; it's death, and Christ had to give us his life to fully cure our hearts of it.

A Tale of Two Disciples

We see the difference between godly grief and worldly grief in the lives of two of the disciples, Peter and Judas. Notice the similarities between the two men. They both followed Jesus; both were considered his disciples; and both heard his teachings and witnessed his miracles. Both men also betrayed him. Judas betrayed his Master for thirty pieces of silver; Peter betrayed him to save his own hide. The reaction of these two men after their sin is exceptionally different. Matthew 27:3–4 states the following concerning Judas:

> Then Judas, his betrayer, seeing that Jesus had been condemned, was full of remorse and returned the thirty pieces of silver to the chief priests and elders. "I have sinned by betraying innocent blood," he said.

The scriptures point out that Judas sinned against God and betrayed Jesus. The scriptures also point out that Judas felt remorse for his actions and even tried to make restitution by returning the money. This remorse did not result in repentance, however, but in a hangman's noose.

Repentance is not just feeling sorry for your sin and making amends; true repentance always leads to Jesus. Judas never made his way back to Jesus, and godly sorrow still leads us back to the cross.

Now, look at Peter. He ran from his master and denied him not once but three times. Luke wrote the following concerning Peter's reaction to his denial: "And he went outside and wept bitterly" (Luke 22:62). We can see the deep emotional turmoil within Peter. Where did his emotions and turmoil lead him? Where did this deep-seated grief lead this broken man?

> Repentance is not just feeling sorry for your sin and making amends; true repentance always leads to Jesus

John 21 records the disciple's full restoration by his Master. Jesus makes his third appearance to his followers as they are fishing. Jesus is preparing a meal for the ones he loves when Peter hears John say that the Lord is on the shore.

> When Simon Peter heard that it was the Lord, he tied his outer clothing around him (for he had taken it off) and plunged into the sea. (John 21:7)

Peter let no obstacle keep him from the Lord. His remorse and repentance led him to an open fire, a breakfast of fish, and the restoring words of Jesus. Jesus asked Peter three times if Peter loved him. He offered Peter three different ways to tell the Lord he loved him, just as he denied him three separate times. Then, in some of the sweetest words from our Lord, "he told him, Follow me" (John 21:19).

Jesus ushered Peter back into the fold with those words: follow me. Repentance leads us there; godly sorrow and grief leads us back to the love of the Lord. Mortification and death of our sin leads us to the one who conquered death through his death on a cross. Derek Thomas writes the following regarding how the mortification of sin shapes who we are in Christ:

> What we need to engage in biblical holiness is a right understanding of who we are. As Ferguson puts it, in order to kill sin; we need to "go back from the point of action to a point from which we can gain energy for the strenuous effort of dealing with sin." We need to go back to the point of our new identity in Christ. We need to ask ourselves, "Who am I?"[22]

What an important question for us to ask. Our identities will either lead to death or life in Christ. To whom do you belong today?

Questions for Personal Reflection

1. What sin are you dealing with currently?
2. How do you practically mortify sin?
3. What is the difference between godly and worldly sorrow?

CHAPTER 24
Grieving Over Lostness

How, then, can they call on him they have not believed in? And how can they believe without hearing about him? And how can they hear without a preacher?
—Romans 10:14

Few things are as important to God as that we, as the church, have lost zeal and passion. We have lost zeal for personal holiness. We have lost enthusiasm for marriage and what it takes to persevere in the midst of personal conflict, differences of opinion, and the rising tide of a noncommittal worldview. We have lost zeal for training others in righteousness, a love of the Word, discipleship of our children, and a host of other identifying marks that have set the people of God apart from the world we occupy.

It's easy to throw stones at and have a negative attitude about the effective ministry of the local church—we don't have to look too far to find a critic. Some people today have left the church and organized religion because of the flaws they see in a local body; they have developed a disdain for the church.

I love the church, I love my local church, I love worshipping with the saints corporately, and I believe the church is the hope of the world. I am a fan of the local church. Kevin DeYoung wrote the following concerning how important it is to be a part of a group of believers, flawed as we may be: "The man who attempts Christianity without the church shoots himself in the foot, shoots his children

> We have to fight against pushing the button on the ejector seat of our faith when we see the flaws in a church or another believer.

in the leg, and shoots his grandchildren in the heart."²³ We have to fight against pushing the button on the ejector seat of our faith when we see the flaws in a church or another believer.

The answer, however, is not in turning a blind eye to the sins of the church. For far too long, we, as believers, have drifted regarding the core foundational convictions that have marked the church for centuries. Any time the Spirit awakens the people of God to a part of God's heart that they have ignored, it's time to repent and embrace the heart of God. Today, many have lost a zeal and passion for sharing the gospel with the lost world surrounding them—or I should say that *I* have lost a zeal and passion for sharing the gospel with the lost world surrounding me. You see, personal change only happens when I hear and obey the Spirit's voice in regard to my sin and blind spots. So a question needs to be asked: when was the last time you grieved the lostness of the community around you?

The Grief of Jesus Over a Lost World

What emotions did our Lord experience while on earth? Have you ever considered this question? We know Jesus was 100 percent human, so he experienced the same emotions we experience—grief, joy, anger, and even anxiety as he approached the cross. Indeed, Jesus was perfect in every way, and his emotions bowed to the Father's will.

Tim Keller makes an interesting observation when it comes to the emotional life of Jesus:

> Over a century ago the great Princeton theologian B.B. Warfield wrote a remarkable scholarly essay called 'The Emotional Life of Our Lord', where he considered every recorded instance in the gospels that described the emotions of Christ. He concluded that by far the most typical statement of Jesus's emotional life was the phrase 'he was moved with compassion,' a Greek phrase that means he was moved from the depths of his being. The Bible records Jesus Christ weeping twenty times for every one time it notes that he laughs.[24]

What can we take from this observation of Jesus in the scriptures? Everyone Jesus ever encountered on earth was lost without him. Stop and ponder this thought for a minute. There was not one single person whom Jesus ate or talked with or healed who was not lost. Everyone in the Old and New Testament, from Moses to the apostle Paul, needed the righteousness of Christ in their lives. The Bible clearly states, "For all have sinned and fall short of the glory of God. They are justified freely by his grace through the redemption that is in Christ Jesus" (Romans 3:23–24).

From the first man to the last infant born, all need the gospel of Jesus Christ and his love. There is no exception, but we often live like God doesn't have to save people. A lot of times we don't see people as lost. We may hold on to the doctrine of salvation—being only through Christ—as one of our core beliefs, but testifying to this doctrine and telling others our belief does not pan out. One of my professors in seminary taught a simple doctrine: take your core beliefs, subtract how you live out these beliefs each day, and you will find what you believe. In other words, we say we believe that Jesus is the only way to heaven, but if we never testify or tell others, then what do we truly believe? Either we think God doesn't mean that "all means all," or we don't believe God will punish sin.

I have seen people witness and share the gospel in foolish and unwise ways—ways that do not reflect the heart of God. With most people, however, the problem is not that we share the gospel in an ineffective or wrong way; the problem is that we seldom share it. I don't mean to sound harsh, but take an inventory of the conversations you had last week. Did you open your mouth and share the story of Jesus? Guess what? As I reflect and write these words, I have to admit I haven't shared either. I'm a pastor; why is it so hard to share the most wonderful news in the world?

I think it's easier than we think, and I don't think the first step is handing out a tract or learning a five-point presentation. Professor of evangelism Alvin Reid states the following concerning the simplicity of sharing the gospel: "Sharing Jesus is as simple as connecting with others around their suffering and their pain."[25] Notice he says nothing about the right strategy or the proper training. Jesus looked upon the

> With most people, however, the problem is not that we share the gospel in an ineffective or wrong way; the problem is that we seldom share it

world, and he has compassion. We are called to do the same, and there is no more compassionate message than the message of the cross. The solution is simple: we must repent of our silence and stop turning a blind eye to the lostness of the world. We must have compassion and go after those far from God with the message of the cross. We will never share the gospel with the lost unless we have compassion for the lost. How do you cultivate a tender heart toward the lost? An excellent place to start is by asking a couple of questions, found in Romans 10:14.

> Jesus looked upon the world, and he has compassion. We are called to do the same, and there is no more compassionate message than the message of the cross.

How Can They Call on Him if They Have Not Believed?

I have always struggled with the tension I feel when I talk to people who go to church and live a decent life yet have no saving concept of Jesus. I have friends who believe there is a God, but they have not placed their faith in Jesus. I have become very comfortable with their positions, and that is a dangerous place. I think I have made people very satisfied with their lack of faith in Christ. Sometimes we get to this place because we don't want to make a person feel uncomfortable, or we don't want to offend a person. I have talked to countless people who have cared for and loved lost family members, coworkers, and friends, but they never acknowledged their lack of faith in Jesus.

We have to ask a tough question, the same question we find in Romans 10:14—can a person have a relationship with God outside of belief in Christ? The answer is a resounding *no*! You might agree with this statement, yet we act like our friends and neighbors are going to get a free pass when it comes to death and eternity. We ignore the warnings concerning the coming judgment of God and even the concept of hell itself. Essentially, the modern church has erased the topic of hell and eternal punishment from our vocabulary. Many see the subject of hell as unloving and unkind, something a loving God would never institute.

We have reshaped the message of the cross to show a kind, loving King who would never punish sin in such a dark place. How can something like hell come from the heart of a kind and loving God? Pastor and author Francis Chan gives insightful and challenging words on this topic:

> It's incredibly arrogant to pick and choose which incomprehensible truths we embrace. No one wants to ditch God's plan of redemption, even though it doesn't make sense to us. Neither should we erase God's revealed plan of punishment because it doesn't sit well with us. As soon as we do this, we are putting God's actions in submission to our reasoning, which is a ridiculous thing to do.[26]

Instead of ignoring the wrath of God and coming judgment, let us embrace grieving hearts over the sin of our world.

Let the lostness of man bring you to your knees in prayer and conviction. Cry over souls, cry out to God over souls, and then pick yourself up and share the powerful story of a crucified Lord, who brings salvation to those condemned in their sin. Don't fool yourself; you can't have a relationship with God unless you believe in the redemption of Jesus.

Use Words and Actions

Several books, magazines, and articles have been written to help churches engage the culture around them. Some are theological, while others give a more pragmatic approach to engaging our neighborhoods. Meeting the needs of a community is one of the ways we engage the culture from a theological and practical point of view. As long as there are humans, there will be needs. The poor, the hungry, the hurt, and the lonely will always be there for us to comfort and engage. The scriptures have constantly called God's people to meet the needs of the world around them.

> Speak up for those who have no voice, for the justice of all who are dispossessed. Speak up, judge righteously, and defend the cause of the oppressed and the needy. (Proverbs 31:8–9)

Jesus tells his disciples,

> Sell your possessions and give to the poor. Make moneybags for yourselves that won't grow old, an inexhaustible treasure in heaven, where no thief comes near and no moth destroys. (Luke 12:33)

God has made it clear where his heart is when it comes to engaging the culture around us. There are needs, and the church should be first in line to meet those needs.

We often fall short of our entire duty. God has not just called us to meet needs; he has called us to meet those needs so that words are spoken—good words, gospel words. Today's church is meeting needs all over the world, but we may stop short of explaining why we are meeting needs. Why *do* we meet needs?

In a world full of greed and individualism, why would a collected group of individuals called Christians meet needs? Because the head of the church met our most significant needs, which was the righteousness needed to stand before God and the blood required to atone for our sins. Every need met and every action done in love should be accompanied by the message of the gospel. Wouldn't it be a tragedy to meet needs here on earth and not tell the story that meets the greatest need?

Our actions have to have words tied to them. Food does not make people believe; clothes do not make people believe. Only the words of the gospel call people to repentance and belief in Christ. We do not choose one or the other; meeting needs and the proclamation of the gospel work hand in hand.

How Will They Believe if We Don't Go?

Paul's final words Romans 10:14 may be the most convicting: "And how can they hear without a preacher?" Most Bible-believing churches answer this question by hiring someone who serves as a preacher. The title *preacher* was given to me by the first church. Many see the preacher as one single individual who preaches a sermon, but a preacher is a proclaimer—one who shares the story of the gospel; one who proclaims the victory Jesus has over sin, the devil, and the grave. Practically, one man cannot accomplish this task; this is a task God has given to all his children. You don't have to be a pastor to be a preacher; you have a story to tell and a testimony to share. The questions are, do you see the lostness around you, and have you experienced the grief it brings to the heart of the Father?

Jesus left the ninety-nine to pursue one, and he calls his church to do the same. Let us do the work of an evangelist and go—sent into a world gripped by sin but open to hearing the story of redemption. When our hearts break over the lost, our feet will swiftly run to them with the gospel.

Questions for Personal Reflection

1. When was the last time you grieved the lost condition of a friend?
2. Why do you think it's so easy to forget about the condition of people who do not have a relationship with Jesus?
3. Why does the proclamation of the gospel involve words and actions?

CHAPTER 25
The Grief of Jesus

> He said to them, "I am deeply grieved to the point of death. Remain here and stay awake with me." Going a little farther, he fell facedown and prayed, "My Father, if it is possible, let this cup pass from me. Yet not as I will, but as you will."
> —Matthew 26:38–39

My mom passed away on June 23, 2014. She developed a glioblastoma tumor in the left hemisphere of her brain. She was homebound when the tumor was discovered and was starting to have some memory issues related to the tumor. We found out in early April; she had surgery right after Easter and lived only ten weeks after the surgery. We prayed fervently for her healing and celebrated after her first surgery when the doctor informed us that he was able to remove a lot of the tumor. Early in the morning, I drove my father to the hospital on the day after her surgery. She had a large white bandage on her head, and we took turns feeding her meals to her. My father was on cloud nine that morning. In his mind, the surgery was a success.

Later in the afternoon, the surgeon made his rounds and spoke to my dad and me, regarding her recovery and future treatment. I didn't understand a lot of the terminology, but one thing he said was very clearly communicated and understood: Mom would be with us on this earth for a maximum of ten months; she lived for ten weeks. It took a while to process the doctor's words concerning my mom's future. We prayed; we prayed for healing. We pleaded with God for success and more days with my mother.

God's will was not for more days; she now rests peacefully with her Lord in heaven.

I have heard my dad pray many prayers, but one of the prayers I will always remember was prayed on the day we found out her disease was terminal. He asked for healing but finally cried out to God, "Not my will but yours." My mom and dad were married for fifty-two years. He never left her side during her last days; he was faithful to the end. We still grieve the death of my mom. My father still becomes emotional when we see an old picture or tell a story about Mom. We all grieve her, but he grieves the most. My grief for my mom will never match the grief my dad experiences. She passed over four years ago, but every day reminds him of the freshness of his loss. On this side of heaven, there will be grief, but grief does not have to define who we are. Our union with Christ defines who we are.

Paul instructs the church concerning their grief with these words: "We do not want you to be uninformed, brothers and sisters, concerning those who are asleep, so you will not grieve like the rest, who have no hope" (1 Thessalonians 4:13). Paul presents two powerful ideas in that passage. First, he acknowledges there will grief in the Christian life, just as there will be pain and suffering. We may feel that God has abandoned us when we grieve, but this is simply how we feel. It is not the truth of the gospel or the truth about the nature of God. God is faithful to the end. He never wavers in his love and commitment to his children, especially in their grief.

We will grieve something in our lives; it may be the death of a beloved spouse or a child. The grief you experience may not be because of natural death; it may be the loss of a job, a dream, or a relationship. The reaction the enemy wants from you is one of hopelessness and despair, but there is always hope in the gospel.

Paul also reminds the church that when we grieve, we grieve with hope. Hope is more than wishful thinking. Hope so much more than trying to make the best of a bad situation. Hope is a light that reminds God's children they are always in the presence of a loving Father. Hope is like a lighthouse shining in the distance, calling weary travelers home, even when the sea roars about them. John Bunyan's classic work, *The Pilgrim's Progress*, was written from a prison cell. The book is a classic allegory of the hard yet grace-filled path the believer walks, which leads to the dwelling place of God and eternal life. Hope, despite circumstances, is a major theme of the book and a major theme of the Christian life. Bunyan wrote the following concerning our Christian journey:

This hill, though high, I covet to ascend; The difficulty will not me offend. For I perceive the way to live lies here. Come, pluck up, heart; let's neither faint nor fear. Better, though difficult, the right way to go, Than wrong, though easy, where the end is woe.[27]

Life is not easy; it's tough and challenging. Grief is not easy—and it's not supposed to be easy. Losing loved ones, dreams, and relationships tears at our hearts and blinds our eyes to the good grace of God, but hope sets our sights on someone greater than our grief.

The Reason We Can Grieve with Hope

We can grieve with hope because of the grief Jesus experiences, as described in Matthew 26:38–39. The cup Jesus refers to in the passage brings us life but takes him to a cross. The cup refers to the wrath of God. God uses the illustration of a cup to give us a picture of his divine wrath.

> This is what the LORD, the God of Israel, said to me, "Take this cup of the wine of wrath from my hand and make all the nations to whom I am sending you to drink from it." (Jeremiah 25:15)

The prophet Ezekiel paints a stunning image of the sin of Israel:

> These things will be done to you because you acted like a prostitute with the nations, defiling yourself with their idols. You have followed the path of your sister, so I will put her cup in your hand. This is what the LORD God says: "You will drink your sister's cup, which is deep and wide. You will be an object of ridicule and scorn." (Ezekiel 23:30–31)

Notice two characteristics in these verses concerning the wrath of God. First, the wrath of God comes from the hand of God. He initiates the pouring of his wrath. Why? Because God is a just and good God who will not turn a blind eye to the sin of humanity. Psalm 89:14 states, "Righteousness and justice are the foundation of your throne." No one cares about justice and righteousness more than God. He will judge the nations and their blatant sin and disobedience to what is right by his eternal decrees and laws.

Second, notice the full cup of God's wrath is drunk, and a drinker is an object of ridicule and scorn. Sin is not something we tame. In the end, sin is death, and sin has consequences. Sin does more than produce shame and guilt; sin brings condemnation. You can be guilty and not have remorse or shame, but you're still guilty and face punishment and condemnation. Not every sin committed by humankind will see the justice that's due on this earth. People have been covering up their sin, running from their sin, and allowing others to take the punishment for their sin since the beginning of time. We may say there is no justice in the world, and this may be an accurate statement. Usually, though, we are thinking of the behavior and sins of others, not our own.

Most people want grace and forgiveness when it comes to their sins, but they want justice and righteousness for the sins of others. Jesus took the weight of the world's sin upon his shoulders and atoned for these sins by his blood. I have marveled at the cross and the empty tomb, but sometimes I need to meditate on the garden. There in the garden, my Lord grieved over the will of God. His grief was deep and sorrowful, yet he yielded his life for mine. God's children no longer bear the guilt and weight of their sin because out of Jesus's grief, obedience was born. He humbled himself and willingly obeyed the will of the Father.

Grief doesn't have to define you. Grief can be an open door to see the hand and the will of God. Grief will shape you, but the gospel can be the mold. We all experience grief; we all experience sorrow. The passing of time will bring grief; our sin and the sins of others will bring grief. Sickness, pain, and heartache will knock on our doors.

> God's children no longer bear the guilt and weight of their sin because out of Jesus's grief, obedience was born.

The difference between the world and the people of God is simple. When grief and sorrow knock at our doors, it is met by a King with nail prints in his hands and feet. The prophet Isaiah painted the most vivid picture of the sorrow and victory of our Lord:

> He didn't have an impressive form or majesty that we should look at him, no appearance that we should desire him. He was despised and rejected by men, a man of suffering who knew what sickness was. He was like someone people turned away from; he was despised, and we didn't value him. Yet he himself bore our sicknesses, and he carried our pains; but we in turn regarded him stricken, struck down by God, and afflicted. But he was pierced because of our rebellion, crushed because of our iniquities; punishment for our peace was on him, and we are healed by his wounds. We all went astray like sheep; we all have turned to our way; and the Lord has punished him for the iniquity of us all. (Isaiah 53:2b-6)

The gospel is highlighted in every word of the prophet's writing, but notice how our Lord accomplished our peace. He did this by himself. Our anger, our grief, our anxiety, and our joy can be lost in the power and might of a God who is a great high priest, who knows the ways of humankind. In Jesus, we find everything we need for this life. Our emotions can now find a safe place in the Savior.

Questions for Personal Reflection

1. Why is grief such a hard emotion to deal with in our lives?
2. How does Jesus identify with us in his grief?
3. How does the gospel shape our grief?

Conclusion

My son likes to draw comic books. He patterns his storylines and illustrations from various sources, mainly professional comic books he finds at the library. He especially likes to hang out in my office and use the copy machine to distribute several issues of his work. As I have been writing, he has been drawing.

One day I was working on one of the chapters for this book, and he asked, "Dad, what is your book about?"

I replied, "It's a book about emotions and how they can get out of hand."

My son looked up from his comic books with his big blue eyes, which get big especially when he is expressing his emotions, and said, "Dad, I need to read that book when you're done. I need help controlling my emotions."

If an eight-year-old can see the need for help with his emotions, then we can admit we need help as well. I want to leave you with four practical principles to remember with regard to how the gospel is applied to our emotional well-being. These principles don't have a "wow factor"; they're simple, but if followed, I believe we can move one step forward in allowing the gospel to control and direct how we respond to the world around us.

Learn to Embrace the Art of Being Silent

We live in a world full of noise and distractions. Since the inception of social media and the technology boom of the early 2000s, humanity has been connected in a virtual world of twenty-four-hour information, news, entertainment, and interaction. Despite having the world at our fingertips, we feel more and more disengaged and, further, disenchanted. So we unplug and unwind. We get off the grid in search of something deeper and meaningful, longing for peace. Often, this involves seeking out a particular place or person. We long to disconnect so that we can reconnect. But what are we looking to reconnect with, and how do we want to reconnect?

It is easy to turn everything off; the problem comes when we are alone in the silence. In the silence, worry and doubt can creep in. Regret and bitterness can sweep over a heart in a matter of minutes. I believe this is why being busy, distracted, and plugged in is so popular—we don't have to face the silence. Believers don't have to dread the silence; they can embrace the silence. Here in the silence, God can speak through the gospel of Jesus Christ in incredible ways. God can use the silence and solitude to shape our emotions, so when we are plugged in and face the day-to-day tasks that generally overwhelm us, we will face them in the confidence of Christ.

How does this work? I have often looked to Proverbs 17:28 for guidance: "Even a fool is considered wise when he keeps silent-discerning, when he seals his lips." Our emotions get us into trouble when they are not anchored in wisdom, discretion, and peace—a word said in anger; an anxious thought that becomes expressions and words of panic; the grief and pain that resound in the silence of an empty house. Our emotions may grow more unstable the further we get away from the truth of the gospel. The silence is where we talk to ourselves the loudest. Discipline yourself in the silence, and your public life will resemble your Lord more than you ever thought.

When you are faced with a situation that makes you angry, learn to embrace the silence. When your thoughts turn anxious and fearful, learn to embrace the silence. When your grief is overwhelming, learn to embrace the silence. In the silence, there is a voice—a voice attached to a person who dwells inside you. He is your teacher, your friend, your confidant, and your advocate. The Holy Spirit will direct and guide you, but you must make room for him to speak. You must sit, be still, and learn to embrace the silence. You don't need a snarky comeback; you don't have to answer every email; you don't have to use your words at every turn.

James teaches us well: "Consider how a small fire sets ablaze a large forest. And the tongue is a fire" (James 3:5–6). How many relationships have been ruined by renegade emotions attached to an ungodly and undisciplined tongue? Sometimes our emotions need to sit in the quiet, under the control of the Holy Spirit, until they are shaped by the gospel and ready to give glory to God, instead of glory to what we are experiencing.

Learn to embrace the silence, give heed to your words, and don't feel you always have to speak.

Fight the Good Fight

One of the goals of this book is to help believers understand their identity in Christ and allow this identity to shape their emotions. Remember, emotions are not bad or sinful. We are emotional creatures; we express ourselves with our emotions. The problem comes when our emotions are shaped more by our sinful hearts than the gospel of Jesus. How does the gospel shape our emotions? I believe this happens when emotions are guarded and protected by the gospel.

Ephesians 6:10–18 gives us believers a blueprint for protecting our emotions. Because we are in Christ, we have his protection, but we have to choose each day to clothe ourselves in his righteousness. Paul uses the imagery of armor to communicate what it means to be clothed in Christ. Why? Because we are in a battle—a battle for our minds, hearts, and hands; a battle for our families, our churches, and the neighborhoods where we live. We battle for each other, and we battle for the glory of Christ, who has equipped us for this good work. Paul highlights five pieces of armor. First, he writes in Ephesians 6:14, "Stand, therefore, with truth like a belt around your waist." When truth clings to us, then our emotions will be based in a gospel truth instead of an imagined possible reality. We may become angry, anxious, or fretful about a situation that has no truth. When we make our emotions face the truth, we can properly respond to the situation we are facing.

Paul writes of "righteousness like armor on your chest." When we respond, knowing that the imputed righteousness of Christ protects us from things in the past, present, and future, then we are free to live the higher spiritual life. We seek the things above. We react like new individuals, not the old. The old individuals are full of rage and fear; the ones who walk in the righteousness of Christ walk in peace and do not fear what will happen. These individuals know who their master is. The old individuals seek joy in this temporal world, and when they can't have the things their hearts desire, their joy is forfeited. The new individuals walk in the joy of the

Lord, understanding that their joy is complete because they have their Lord forever. The righteousness of Christ protects our hearts fully.

Ephesians 6:15 says, "And your feet sandaled with readiness for the gospel of peace." We can't get away from our emotions. We may try to stuff our emotions deep down inside, a kind of stoic way to control them, but the problem with stuffing our emotions is that one day, they will come to the surface—often more out of control than when we stuffed them. We carry our emotions around, even the ones we ignore, yet Christians have the gospel of peace as they journey. This gospel brings peace to relationships and to environments, and it brings inner peace. When we have the peace of the gospel, our emotions can experience the peace that only the Son of Man brings.

Not only do we have this gospel of peace, but we have the shield of faith, which can be used in any situation. Paul describes the shield with these words: "Take up the shield of faith with which you can extinguish all the flaming arrows of the evil one" (Ephesians 6:16). Armies would dip their arrows in tar and shoot flaming arrows at their enemies, so armies had to learn to fight as one unit. Roman shields were made so a soldier was protected from his neckline to just below his knees. Soldiers learned to fight shoulder to shoulder, with the front line protecting the lines in the rear. A well-trained unit could take an onslaught of arrows because they fought together.

This is the way God's children engage in spiritual warfare. We are not loners; we fight shoulder to shoulder. We care about each other, and we face the enemy together. We care about the anxious thoughts and fears of our brothers. We grieve together with our sisters, and we experience the joy of God together as a church, awaiting the coming day of our Lord.

Finally, Paul instructs the church to take up "the helmet of salvation, and the sword of the Spirit-which is the word of God" (Ephesians 6:17). Our minds are not controlled by the flesh, as we have the mind of Christ—the mind of a servant, the mind of an obedient son who joyfully desires to do the will of his Father in heaven. Our minds are protected by this great salvation, allowing us to think clearly on heavenly things—things that transcend this temporal place—but that echo the chorus of heaven. This salvation directs our lives and helps us to wield the Word of God, faithfully and accurately. We live by this Word and use it to strike at an enemy who would play on our emotions. When we suit up, our emotions can be protected so they can be shaped by the gospel of Christ.

Lay Your Emotions at the Foot of the Cross

Paul wrote the following: "For the word of the cross is foolishness to those who are perishing, but it is the power of God to us who are being saved" (1 Corinthians 1:18). I don't know many who want their emotions to run their lives. Not many of us enjoying being angry or anxious. Grief can grip our lives so hard that it feels like we are the ones who are lost. Misplaced joy can cause us to make unwise and sinful decisions. Our emotions need a resting place, and this place is at the foot of the cross.

At first, this sounds foolish, and this is what the world would say: how can an instrument of death bring power and life? We only find life when we allow the power of the cross to guide our lives. Otherwise, we too perish. One of the most important and practical disciplines a believer can practice is daily laying their hopes, dreams, desires, and emotions at the foot of the cross. Here, we find peace, and here, we find hope. At the foot of the cross, our anger is laid to rest, replaced by peace. At the foot of the cross, our anxiety faces a King who is sovereign over all the things that make us fearful. He has conquered death and the grave through the cross; therefore, what is there to fear? Our grief is not grief that consumes but that ends with hope—the hope of a home with a faithful King, who paid the price for his children. And our joy is fully realized in the love of Christ. Our emotions are only at home when they are at home with Jesus. So lay your emotions down at the feet of the one who has control over them.

Endnotes

1. C. J. Mahaney, *Living the Cross Centered Life* (New York: Multnomah, 2006), 132.
2. Paul Tripp, *Instruments in the Redeemer's Hands* (Phillipsburg: P&R Publishing, 2002), 47.
3. C. S. Lewis, *The Four Loves* (New York: Harcourt, Brace, Jovanovich, 1960), 169–170.
4. Robert Alden, *The Expositor's Bible Commentary: Habakkuk* (Grand Rapids: Zondervan, 1985), 533.
5. John Rosemond, *The Well-Behaved Child* (Thomas Nelson, 2009), 9.
6. John Piper, *When I Don't Desire God* (Wheaton: Crossway Books, 2004), 81.
7. C. J. Mahaney, *Living the Cross Centered Life* (New York: Multnomah, 2006), 132.
8. Paul Tripp, *New Morning Mercies: A Gospel Devotional* (Wheaton: Crossway Books, 2019), 35.
9. David Garland, *I Corinthians: Baker Exegetical Commentary of the New Testament* (Grand Rapids: Baker Academic, 2003), 9.
10. Paul Tripp, *Suffering: Gospel Hope When Life Doesn't Make Sense* (Wheaton: Crossway Books, 2018), 29.
11. Jon Stott, *The Cross of Christ* (Downers Grove: Intervarsity Press, 2006), 37.
12. J. D. Greear, *Stop Asking Jesus into Your Heart* (Nashville: B&H Publishing Group, 2013), 5.
13. Derek Thomas, *How the Gospel Brings Us All the Way Home* (Orlando: Reformation Trust, 2011), xiii.
14. Timothy Keller, *The Meaning of Marriage* (New York: The Penguin Group, 2011), 109.
15. C. S. Lewis, *The Four Loves* (New York: Harper Collins, 1960), 155.
16. David Kessler, *On Grief and Grieving* (New York: Scribner Publishing, 2004), 4.
17. C. S. Lewis, *A Grief Observed* (Sydney: Harper Collins, 1996), 70.
18. Timothy Keller, *Walking with God through Pain and Suffering* (New York: The Penguin Group, 2013), 29.
19. C. S. Lewis, *A Grief Observed* (Sydney: Harper Collins, 1996), 6.
20. John Piper, *Desiring God: Meditations of a Christian Hedonist* (Colorado Springs: Multnomah Books, 2003), 12.

21 John Owen, *The Mortification of Sin* (Apollo: Ichthus Publications, 2014), 14.
22 Derek Thomas, *How the Gospel Brings Us All the Way Home* (Orlando: Reformation Trust, 2011), 51.
23 Kevin DeYoung, *The Hole in Our Holiness* (Wheaton: Crossway Books, 2012), 132.
24 Timothy Keller, *The Prodigal Prophet* (New York: The Penguin Group, 2018), 109.
25 Alvin Reid, *Sharing Jesus without Freaking Out* (Nashville: B&H Academic, 2017), 2.
26 Francis Chan, *Erasing Hell* (Colorado Springs: David Cook, 2011), 136.
27 John Bunyan, *The Pilgrim's Progress* (New York: Washington Square Press, 1957), 46.

About the Author

Dr. Kevin Wilson serves as the Pastor of Spiritual Growth for Fellowship Community Church, a multi-site church located in the heart of the Roanoke Valley in Virginia. He has written two bible studies, "The Holy Spirit: Seeing the Power of God Unleashed in Your Life", and "Hope is Here: A Study in John 16-20. He holds a D.Min in Expository Preaching from The Southern Baptist Theological Seminary in Louisville, Kentucky. Dr. Wilson lives in the Roanoke Valley with his wife Kristina and two children, Anna Kate and Parker.